Cracking the
SAT*

French Subject Test

2009–2010 Edition

Cracking the

SAT*

French Subject Test

2009–2010 Edition

Monique Gaden and Simone Ingram

PrincetonReview.com

Random House, Inc. New York

The Princeton Review, Inc.
2315 Broadway
New York, NY 10024
E-mail: editorialsupport@review.com

ISBN 978-0-375-42907-1
ISSN 1075-6051

Editor: Selena Coppock
Production Editor: Emma Parker
Production Coordinator: Ryan Tozzi

Printed in the United States of America.

10 9 8 7 6 5 4 3 2 1

2009–2010 Edition

John Katzman, Chairman, Founder
Michael J. Perik, President, CEO
Stephen Richards, COO, CFO
John Marshall, President, Test Preparation Services
Rob Franek, VP Test Prep Books, Publisher

Editorial
Seamus Mullarkey, Editorial Director
Laura Braswell, Senior Editor
Rebecca Lessem, Senior Editor
Selena Coppock, Editor
Heather Brady, Editor

Production Services
Scott Harris, Executive Director, Production Services
Kim Howie, Senior Graphic Designer

Production Editorial
Meave Shelton, Production Editor
Emmeline Parker, Production Editor

Research & Development
Ed Carroll, Agent for National Content Directors
Liz Rutzel, Project Editor

Random House Publishing Team
Tom Russell, Publisher
Nicole Benhabib, Publishing Manager
Ellen L. Reed, Production Manager
Alison Stoltzfus, Associate Managing Editor
Elham Shabahat, Publishing Assistant

Acknowledgments

Thank you to Benjamin Young, Faculty Fellow at Columbia University, for his additional input on changes in the Vocabulary and Grammar sections of this book.

Special thanks to Adam Robinson, who conceived of and perfected the Joe Bloggs approach to standardized tests and many of the other successful techniques used by The Princeton Review.

Thank you to Mindy Myers for her comprehensive review of this text for the 2009–2010 edition.

Contents

Part I
Orientation

Chapter 1
Introduction

You have chosen to take the SAT French Subject Test, and now it is time to demonstrate all you have learned during the course of your advanced study. This book will help you understand the format of the SAT French Test and will give you all the tools you need to do your best.

This book is divided into four parts: Part One gives you an orientation of the French Subject Test and reveals some basic strategies. Part Two gives you the format for each section of the test and reviews key grammar and vocabulary words. Part Three contains answers and explanations for the drills found in Part Two. Part Four contains two practice SAT French Subject Tests along with answers and explanations for each test.

What Are the SAT Subject Tests?

They are a series of one-hour exams developed and administered by the Educational Testing Service (ETS) and the College Board. The SAT Subject Tests are designed to measure specific knowledge in specific areas. There are many different tests in many different subject areas, such as biology, history, French, and math. They are scored separately on a 200–800 scale.

How Are SAT Subject Tests Used by College Admissions?

Because the tests are given in specific areas, colleges use them as another piece of admissions information and, often, to decide whether an applicant can be exempted from college requirements. A good SAT French score might place you in second-year French instead of first-year French, or exempt you from a foreign language requirement altogether.

Should I Take the SAT Subject Tests? How Many? When?

About one-third of the colleges that require SAT scores also require that you take two or three Subject Tests. Your first order of business is to start reading those college catalogs. College guidebooks, admissions offices, and guidance counselors should have this information as well.

As to which tests you should take, the answer is simple:

1. Those Subject Tests that you will do well on, and
2. The tests that the colleges you are applying to may require you to take.

The best possible situation, of course, is when the two overlap.

Some colleges have specific requirements, others do not. Again, start asking questions before you start taking tests. Once you find out which tests are required, if any, part of your decision making is done. The next step is to find out which of the tests will highlight your particular strengths.

Possibilities range from math, English literature, U.S. or world history, biology, chemistry, and physics to a variety of foreign languages.

As to when you should take the tests, schedule them as close as possible to the corresponding coursework you may be doing. If you plan to take the SAT Chemistry Subject Test, for example, and you are currently taking chemistry in high school, don't postpone the test until next year.

When Are the SAT Subject Tests Offered?

In general, you can take from one to three Subject Tests per test date in October, November, December, January, May, and June at test sites across the country. Not all subjects are offered at each administration, so check the dates carefully.

How Do I Register for the Tests?

To register by mail, pick up a registration form and student bulletin at your guidance office. You can also register at the College Board website at www.collegeboard.com. This site contains other useful information such as the test dates and fees. If you have questions, you can talk to a representative at the College Board by calling 1-609-771-7600.

You may have your scores sent to you, to your school, and to four colleges of your choice. Additional reports will be sent to additional colleges for—you guessed it—additional money. Scores are made available to students via the College Board's website roughly three weeks after the test date. Results are usually mailed out about 7 to 10 days after they are released online.

Score Choice is Back!

Beginning in February 2009, you will be able to choose which SAT Subject Test scores you want colleges to see. This is great news! For one thing, if you take more than one SAT Subject Test on a given test date, you'll be able to choose which tests from that date you'd like to submit to colleges. So if, for example, you take the French test followed by the chemistry test, but don't think the chemistry test went very well, you can simply opt out of having that chemistry score sent to your schools. Also, while the changes will go into effect beginning with the March 2009 SAT test date (the new policy applies to both the SAT and SAT Subject Tests), you'll be allowed to use the new feature retroactively for scores prior to March 2009. If you have an older subject test score from freshman year, say, that isn't as good as you'd like, you'll be able to choose not to send it out to colleges.

The new score reporting policy, as it's being called, will be optional for students. This means that you aren't required to opt in and actively choose which specific scores you would like sent to colleges. If you decide not to use the new score-reporting feature, then all of the scores on file will automatically be sent when you request score reports.

For more information about the new score-reporting policy, go to the College Board website at www.collegeboard.com.

What's a Good Score?

That's hard to say, exactly. A good score is one that fits in the range of scores the college of your choice usually accepts or looks for. However, if your score falls below the normal score range for Podunk University, that doesn't mean you won't get into Podunk University. Schools are usually fairly flexible in what they are willing to look at as a "good" score for a particular student.

Along with your score, you will also receive a percentile rank. That number tells you how you fit in with the other test takers. In other words, a percentile rank of 60 means that 40 percent of the test takers scored above you and 60 percent scored below you.

What Is The Princeton Review?

The Princeton Review is a test-preparation company based in New York City. We have branches across the country and abroad. We've developed the techniques you'll find in our books, courses, and online resources by analyzing actual exams and testing their effectiveness with our students. What makes our techniques unique is that we base our principles on the same ones used by the people who write the tests. We don't want you to waste your time with superfluous information; we'll give you just the information you'll need to get great score improvements. You'll learn to recognize and comprehend the relatively small amount of information that's actually tested. You'll also learn to avoid common traps, to think like the test writers, to find answers to questions you're unsure of, and to budget your time effectively.

You need to do only two things: trust the techniques, and practice, practice, practice.

The College Board publishes a book called *The Official Study Guide for all SAT Subject Tests* with practice exams for all 20 SAT subjects offered. You can also go to the College Board website, www.collegeboard.com, for more information and practice questions. After you have worked through the review chapters and completed the practice tests in this book, try out your new skills on real SAT Subject Test questions.

What Makes This Book Different?

Most prep books for foreign language tests are written by academics who ramble on about the subtleties of the syntax of their chosen languages. Their cups runneth over with more rules and reasons about grammar than you could ever absorb in a limited period of time. Most of all, they take more interest in teaching you French with a capital F than in preparing you for the particular challenges of this test. Rather than waste your time—as other prep books do—rehashing every tedious rule of grammar, we'll cover only those points needed to get you a good score on the test. We want you to study effectively. What you do with your French on your own time is your business.

Some prep books can harm you more than help you by misleading you about the types of questions or by giving you so much to review that you don't know where to begin or what's most important. In our 20 years of test-prep experience, we've learned what you truly need to know to score your best.

What Is the SAT French Subject Test?

You can choose to take one of the two French Subject Tests: French or French with Listening. While the French Subject Test is generally offered on every SAT Subject Test date (except November), French with Listening is only given in November. It has an additional audio portion, which evaluates your ability to comprehend spoken French. You listen to a recording and answer multiple-choice questions. If you intend to continue your French language study, this is useful for placement purposes. You are not tested on your speaking or writing ability on either of these tests.

Will Slang or Casual Expressions Be Included on the Test?

Only authentic and widely accepted French language is used on the test. The SAT French is testing what should have been taught in a minimum of two years of regular French study in high school. Of course, the more you study, the better your scores will be.

What Does It Test?

The SAT French tests vocabulary, reading comprehension, and a few points of grammar. A strong vocabulary will help you score well on the Vocabulary and Reading Comprehension sections. Our review groups words by category for easier recall and gives you tips for learning vocabulary.

As you probably know, French grammar is complex, but the SAT French Subject Test only tests you on a small portion of all grammar. You do not need to know spelling, where the accents go, or correct word order in a sentence. You don't need to know how to conjugate the *passé simple* or the imperfect of the subjunctive. We'll review only those points of grammar that serve you best on the test.

You can't master all of the French language in a few weeks or even a month. Focus on the vocabulary and grammar that helps you on the test.

Now for the Good News

In the scheme of standardized tests, the SAT French isn't all bad. Any standardized test provides you with a wealth of opportunity. Wouldn't you rather take a test in which you can use the Process of Elimination and guessing techniques than walk into a room and speak to a French person? By using an approach that has been developed over the years at The Princeton Review, you'll have the confidence and the ability to ace the SAT French Subject Test.

How Is the SAT French Subject Test Scored?

The scoring system for the SAT French Test is similar to that for the SAT. You are given a raw score based on the number of questions you got right minus one-third of a point for every wrong answer. The raw score is then converted to a scaled score ranging from 200 to 800.

Your SAT French score may be used to place you into the appropriate level of French class in college. If you score well, you may be able to take fewer semesters of language class. If you score really well, you may be exempted from the language requirement completely.

How Will I Improve My Score?

Unfortunately, reading through this book may not be enough. It is important that you apply our techniques during the practice sections so that our approach will be second nature when you take the actual test.

Read one section of the book at a time and immediately apply what you have learned to the practice section that follows it. Then, carefully read through the explanations, looking for patterns in the mistakes that you made. If you notice that one type of question or topic is giving you trouble, go back and review the relevant section. Finally, before taking the diagnostic test at the back of the book, review both the general test-taking strategies and the specific question strategies. Again, after taking the test, notice where your mistakes were, and use that information to adjust your pacing and intensify your review.

Although this book can be used alone, you may find it handy to have a French/English dictionary and a grammar book available as references while you read through the text. Don't use them on the practice tests, though!

This book is designed to help you focus on those points that will help you score higher. It assumes that you have a basic French vocabulary and a rough grasp of grammar. The grammar section highlights the rules that are actually tested, giving you a concise explanation of each rule and examples of test questions. If you are someone who likes detailed explanations, you may want to have your school grammar book handy to use alongside this review book.

> For more information visit www.PrincetonReview.com.

Chapter 2
General Strategy

In this chapter, we'll discuss the best way for you to approach the SAT French Subject Test. Pacing, Process of Elimination, and knowing when or whether to guess are all important factors that can determine how many points you accumulate as you work. You will also get a first look at the structure of the exam so you can plan your study time accordingly. Good luck!

HOW TO IMPROVE

As on any multiple-choice standardized test, you can learn to leverage your knowledge into the best possible score by following a few simple principles.

Attitude

Do not be intimidated by the test! This is only a test that stamps you with a number so that you can be easily classified by the colleges to which you apply. It measures some vocabulary, some minor rules such as which phrases take the subjunctive, and, above all, how well you do on standardized tests.

We can't make up for what you did or didn't learn in school, but we can teach you to make the most of what you do know and boost your test-taking savvy. We'll teach you new ways of approaching the test: pacing yourself, spotting wrong answers, and using guessing skills that put you in control.

Pacing

Standardized tests aren't like school tests. They are actually designed so that hardly anyone can finish all the questions. Don't stress about answering every question or getting through the entire test.

In school, most of us were trained to answer every question on a test. That made sense because those tests were usually written so that there was time to answer every question. On standardized tests, such thinking can lower your score. These tests are designed so that 99 percent of the population cannot finish the test without rushing and making careless mistakes. Slowing down—finding a pace at which you can work carefully and confidently—is the first step to improving your score. Remember, you are not given a negative score on a question you left unanswered.

There is no advantage to answering all the questions on a test if you answer so hurriedly that you get most of them wrong. Think of each question as an investment in your score. Take enough time to make the work you put in pay off in terms of points. Most people don't realize that they can get a terrific score by doing fewer questions. While this philosophy holds true for all standardized tests, it is especially important for the SAT Subject Tests, in which one-third of a point is deducted for each wrong answer.

One caution: Working slowly and carefully is great. Spending five minutes to get an answer on a single question is not. Don't let your pride keep you struggling with a question that's giving you a hard time; each question has the same value. Do what you can, eliminate wrong answer choices, and guess. Then move on to a new question.

You'll have one hour to work on the entire test. You are not timed on each section. That means you can spend less time on sections that you are stronger in, or just move at a steady, careful pace through the whole test.

Work for Accuracy, Not for Speed

The scoring system used by the College Board rewards you for slowing down. It is better to do fewer questions well than to do many questions badly.

The following guide tells you approximately how many questions you have to answer to get a particular score. (This is the approximate number you should answer—not counting guesses—making no more than five errors.) Keep in mind that the scale changes each year, depending on the difficulty of the exam.

To get this score:	Answer this many questions (out of 85):
500	25
550	35
600	45
650	55
700	65
750	75
800	85

So, to get a 600 you have to answer barely half of the test. You can skip the questions that give you the most trouble.

As you do each practice section, you can check your pacing by comparing the number you got right with the number you got wrong. If you made more than two careless errors in that section (not counting guesses), you may want to slow down and attempt fewer questions on the practice test.

You could skip as many as 20 questions and still score a 700.

Which Ones Should You Skip?

On Parts A and B, the questions are arranged roughly in order of increasing difficulty, so unless you are aiming for more than a 600, you may skip the last third of each part. On Parts C and D, there is no clear order of difficulty. Skip questions you don't like and spend time on those you do.

You don't have to answer the same proportion of questions on each part. For most people, reading comprehension is the most difficult and vocabulary is the easiest. If that's true for you, do extra vocabulary and fewer reading-comprehension questions.

Tailor your pacing strategy to your strengths and weaknesses. If your reading ability is strong and your grammar is weak, pace yourself accordingly.

Process of Elimination

No matter how good you are at French, you may still come across a question or two that will stump you. What can you do? Look for obviously incorrect answers, and get rid of them. It is often easier to find three wrong answers than it is to find one right one. If the sentence completion has something to do with going to the beach, an answer choice that means "pincushion" is probably not what you're looking for. The College Board also has some favorite ways to trap test takers who aren't completely sure of themselves. Once you know how they trick you, you're protected from falling into that trap and you're one answer choice closer to the correct one. On some occasions, you may even be able to eliminate all but the correct choice.

Only Make Smart Guesses

Random vs. Educated Guessing
Make a distinction between random guessing and educated guessing. Random guessing (when you have no clue at all) won't help your score. Educated guessing (when you know enough to eliminate at least one answer choice) boosts your score.

Eliminate as many of the wrong answer choices as possible, then guess. The way the test is scored, you get one point for each right answer and you only lose a fraction of a point for the wrong answers. You should skip the question if you really have no clue. However, if you can eliminate even one or two answer choices, it's to your advantage to guess. If you're down to two choices and can't decide, guess and move on to the next question.

OVERALL STRUCTURE OF THE TEST

The SAT French Subject Test consists of four types of multiple-choice questions. You are free to work on the sections or questions in any order that you choose. You will have 60 minutes to answer 85 questions.

The layout of each test will look something like this:

- Part A—Vocabulary Completions
  (approx. 20–26 questions)
- Part B—Grammar Blanks
  (approx. 15–20 questions)
- Part C—Paragraph Blanks
  (approx. 12–20 questions)
- Part D—Reading Comprehension
  (approx. 27 questions)

The exact breakdown of questions will vary from test to test. The list above gives you the approximate number of each type of question.

If Reading Comprehension contains "schedules and tickets" questions as well as traditional passages, then Reading Comprehension will have more questions and Grammar will have slightly fewer.

Part II
Subject Review

Chapter 3
Vocabulary

This chapter gives you several techniques to boost your score on Part A of the SAT French Test. First, get acquainted with the format and structure of the vocabulary section of the test. If you understand how the test writers think, you can get a question right even if you don't know the answer. Then you'll learn additional strategies that will get you more points—tactics to use depending on how well you understand the question. What do you do if you are not sure of the answer? What if you do not know the meaning of the sentence? What if you do not know all the words in the answer choices? Just follow the simple steps we give you, and you'll be ready to handle any of these situations.

PART A: VOCABULARY COMPLETIONS

The first part of the test consists of approximately 20 to 26 vocabulary completions. Each question is a sentence containing a blank. Each of the four answer choices provides a word that could fill in the blank. The correct answer is the one that best completes the sentence in terms of the meaning of the word. (All choices will be grammatically correct.)

Here are the directions for this section as they appear on the test. Become familiar with these directions now so that you don't waste valuable time when you take the test.

Part A

> **Directions:** This part consists of a number of incomplete statements, each having four suggested completions. Select the most appropriate completion and fill in the corresponding oval on the answer sheet.

If your vocabulary needs work, short, frequent study sessions will help you more than long, infrequent ones. Your brain will only be able to absorb a small amount of information at a time. Ten minutes a day between now and the test will make a big difference.

The questions are arranged roughly in order of difficulty.

WHAT MAKES THE DIFFERENCE IN THIS SECTION?

Vocabulary, vocabulary, vocabulary. If your vocabulary is not strong, start working on it right away. In Chapter 4, Vocabulary Review, there are several techniques designed to boost your vocabulary.

Drill 1

Test your vocabulary by writing the English translations of the following words. Answers can be found in Chapter 8.

une usine _____

la honte _____

l'oeuvre _____

en vouloir à _____

mou _____

taquiner _____

la foule _____

ramasser _____

soutenir _____

repasser _____

se méfier de _____

se débarrasser de _____

If you missed more than three of the words, you may need to give vocabulary work extra attention (Chapter 4).

IF YOU KNOW THE WORDS

Fill in Your Own Word

As you read through the sentence, fill in your own word in English **before you look** at the answer choices. Cover the answer choices with your hand, if need be.

> Le film était tellement amusant qu'elle . . . sans cesse.

If something is funny, what does someone do?

Now let's look at the answer choices and see which one is closest to the English answer you decided on:

    (A) dansait
    (B) mangeait
    (C) riait
    (D) lisait

If you thought of the word "laughed" or "smiled," you can eliminate *dansait*, which means "danced," *mangeait*, which means "ate," and *lisait*, which means "read." The correct answer is *riait*, "laughed."

If you understand most of the words in the question, you'll have no problem filling in the blank.

Cover the answer choices and fill in a word for the following examples.

> Jean-Pierre a mal . . . parce qu'il a trop mangé.

    (A) à l'oreille
    (B) au ventre
    (C) aux genoux
    (D) à la tête

If someone ate too much, he would probably have a pain in the "belly." You could then eliminate (A), which means "the ear," (C), which means "the knees," and (D), which means "the head." Choice (B), meaning "the abdomen," is the correct answer.

> La banque se trouve . . . le supermarché et la poste.

    (A) dans
    (B) sur
    (C) pendant
    (D) entre

The word in the blank should give the position of the bank in relationship to the supermarket and the post office: "between" or "near." You can eliminate (A), which means "inside," (B), which means "on," and (C), which means "during." Choice (D), which means "between," is the correct answer.

Watch Out for Trap Answers

Don't immediately pick the first word that seems right. Look at all the answer choices, and leave in only those that might work. Then carefully compare the remaining choices before selecting an answer.

> Si tu n'as pas assez d'argent pour acheter le livre,
> tu peux le trouver à . . .
>
> (A) la librairie
> (B) l'épicerie
> (C) la bibliothèque
> (D) la papeterie

If you don't have enough money to buy a book, you will probably go to a "library." If you know the vocabulary, you might immediately identify the right answer. If not, eliminate (B), which means "grocery store," and (D), which means "stationery store." Is the answer *librairie* or *bibliothèque?* Which means "library?" The answer in this case is the less obvious one: (C), *bibliothèque.* *Librairie* means "bookstore." See page 57 for "Common Mix-Ups."

On average, each Part A section contains one question that tests your knowledge of words for body parts and one question that tests the words for different types of stores.

IF YOU DON'T KNOW ALL THE ANSWER CHOICES

Sometimes you'll be able to fill in a word, but you won't be sure which answer choice matches the word you picked. The following guessing techniques will improve your odds of picking the correct answer.

Use Process of Elimination (POE)

First, clear out the obviously wrong options. Eliminate answer choices that you are sure do not match the word you chose. With the remaining choices, try to guess what each means.

Use Your English

Although it is your knowledge of French that is being tested, your own native language can often help you. Many English words are derived from French, so it makes sense that some words are nearly identical in both languages (but, again, watch out for those traps). How hard is it to guess what *régulier* means? *Transporter? Bière?*

Drill 2

Decide what English words the following French words remind you of: Answers can be found in Chapter 8.

évaluer   _____

sacré   _____

retarder   _____

fréquenter   _____

nombre   _____

assurer   _____

raison   _____

plante   _____

attraper   _____

servir   _____

content   _____

accord   _____

cru   _____

Using English can help you make an educated guess about the meaning of a word. Based on that guess, you can decide to keep the word or eliminate it, narrowing the field of choices and improving your odds. Don't automatically pick the first word that reminds you of the English word you are looking for.

Use this technique with caution on hard questions. On difficult questions (especially the last five questions), use this technique only to eliminate wrong choices, not to pick the right answer. On tough questions, if an answer choice reminds you strongly of the word you're looking for in English, it's practically guaranteed that it's a trap answer.

On easy questions (the first third of the section), the right answer will not be a tough vocabulary word. On hard questions (the final third), the right answer will not be the answer that reminds you of the word in English that you are looking for.

27. ------- des étudiants sortant de l'école a rompu le silence du quartier.

    (A) Le martelage
    (B) La chatière
    (C) Le ramassage
    (D) Le bavardage

This is a tough question. If you understand the sentence ("The _____ of the students leaving school broke the silence in the neighborhood."), you know you're looking for a word that means noise, talk, or chatter. Even if you weren't sure of the whole sentence, you might have seen "silence" and known that you were looking for a word that relates to silence. Which answer is a trap?

Choice (B) looks like the English word "chatter." Since this is a hard question (from the final third), you know it's a trap. *La chatière* actually means "the ventilation hole." The correct answer is (D), which means "the chatting." (A) means "the hammering" (*un marteau* is a hammer), and (C) means "the gathering." On difficult questions, don't pick the answer that reminds you of the word you're looking for in English.

On hard questions, be wary of trap answers but don't psych yourself out! If you know the meaning of all the words, the right answer is still the right answer. Don't cross off the right answer because you're afraid it's too "obvious." Trap answers have a specific feel to them.

Find as many opportuni-
ties as possible to hear
and speak French. Check
your TV or radio guides for
programs in French, rent
French movies, and go
to websites in French,
such as:
www.tv5.fr
www.rfi.fr
www.lemonde.fr

Look for Easier Versions of Words

On difficult questions (or if your vocabulary isn't very strong), you can sometimes figure out an easier version of the answer choices. For example, in the verb *feuilleter* you may see the word *feuille*, meaning "leaf" or "sheet of paper." Could there be a verb meaning "to leaf"? Yes, just as in English, you can "leaf" through a book.

What easier words do you see in the following words?

prochainement   _____

emporter   _____

parapluie   _____

retarder   _____

Well? In *prochainement,* you probably saw *prochain*, which means "next," so *prochainement* probably has something to do with being next. (It means "in a short while" or "coming up next.") You probably see *porter*, which means "to carry," in *emporter*, so you might be able to guess that *emporter* has a similar meaning. It means "to carry away." And what about *parapluie*? Recognize the word *pluie*, "rain"? So *parapluie* is likely to be "umbrella." *Retarder* has the word *tard,* or "late," in it, so it's a safe bet that *retarder* means "to slow or delay."

Avoid Look-Alike Answers

The College Board sometimes tries to trick you by providing answers that look like either the correct answer or a word that appeared in the sentence.

Je dois réparer ma montre; elle ne . . . plus.

(A) casse
(B) montre
(C) donne
(D) marche

If something needs to be fixed, what doesn't it do anymore? Most likely, it doesn't work. Which answer choice means "to work"? Answer choice (B) is a look-alike trap here. *Montre,* meaning "show," is identical to the word *montre*, meaning "wristwatch," in the sentence. It's a trap! Eliminate it. The correct answer is (D) *marche.* The verb *marcher* used with an inanimate object means "to work or function correctly."

IF YOU DON'T UNDERSTAND THE SENTENCE

Word Association

Even if you're shaky on the exact meaning of the sentence, you can still make an educated guess for the answer. Go through the words in the sentence that you do know and see if any of the answer choices are in some way associated with those words.

You often don't need the whole sentence to figure out what word you're looking for. Usually one or two key words in the sentence point to the answer.

Drill 3

For the following incomplete questions, pick the answer choice that makes the most sense given the words that are shown.

Answers can be found in Chapter 8.

xxxxxxxx xxxxxxxx *légumes* xxxx xxxxx . . .
        vegetables

(A) cheminée
(B) jardin
(C) gazon
(D) quartier

xx xxxx xxxxxxx x *tombé* xxx xxxx . . .
        fallen

(A) envolée
(B) échappée
(C) cassée
(D) attrapée

xx xx x xxx xxxxx *chaises* xxxx . . . xxxx xx xxxxx.
        chairs

(A) assommer
(B) s'asseoir
(C) assurer
(D) associer

xxxxx xxxx *ne se sent pas bien* xxxxx xxx . . .
        doesn't feel well

(A) une fièvre
(B) une armoire
(C) un verger
(D) une annonce

xxxxx xxxx xxxxxxxxx xxxxx *mangé* xxx xxx . . .
        eaten

(A) soutenir
(B) emporter
(C) avaler
(D) évaluer

Practice Section

Answers can be found in Chapter 8.

Part A

Directions: This part consists of a number of incomplete statements, each having four suggested completions. Select the most appropriate completion and fill in the corresponding oval on the answer sheet.

1. Il fait froid dehors. Est-ce que toutes les . . . sont fermées?
   - (A) chambres
   - (B) cheminées
   - (C) fenêtres
   - (D) notes

2. Ne fais pas de bruit; les enfants sont . . .
   - (A) venus
   - (B) endormis
   - (C) partis
   - (D) tristes

3. Est-ce que ces fleurs sont de votre . . . ?
   - (A) peinture
   - (B) garage
   - (C) jardin
   - (D) verger

4. Ce manteau n'a pas de . . . où mettre mon porte-monnaie.
   - (A) manches
   - (B) portes
   - (C) poches — pockets
   - (D) monnaie

5. Jeanne s'est réveillée . . . pour voir le lever du soleil.
   - (A) bas
   - (B) haut
   - (C) tard
   - (D) tôt

6. Le train est parti . . . à midi.
   - (A) du garage
   - (B) du toit
   - (C) de l'histoire
   - (D) de la gare

7. Au repas du dimanche, nous mangeons un . . . avec des pommes de terre.
   - (A) rôti
   - (B) ruban
   - (C) régime
   - (D) rôle

8. Les tartes qui sont vendues dans cette . . . sont délicieuses.
   - (A) pâtisserie
   - (B) pharmacie
   - (C) épicerie
   - (D) librairie

9. Tu peux te laver maintenant. La salle de bains est . . .
   - (A) gratuite
   - (B) libre
   - (C) livrée
   - (D) seule

10. Mon . . . pour la classe est de traduire un poème de Rimbaud.
    - (A) destin
    - (B) composition
    - (C) droit
    - (D) devoir

11. Le bruit dans un club peut être tellement fort qu'on a mal . . .

    (A) aux oreilles
    (B) aux orteils
    (C) à l'orgueil
    (D) à la gorge

12. La lune est si . . . que je ne peux pas imaginer que l'homme y soit allé.

    (A) longue
    (B) fade
    (C) loin
    (D) immense

13. Ce n'est pas nécessaire de sortir la poubelle; Jean l'a . . . fait. *present tense*

    (A) hier
    (B) ce matin
    (C) déjà
    (D) d'un côté

14. Nous passerons Noël avec mes grands-parents . . .

    (A) cet été
    (B) cet automne
    (C) cet hiver
    (D) ce printemps

15. Vous avez déjà fait vos devoirs? Cela . . .

    (A) m'admet
    (B) me fait mal
    (C) me trompe
    (D) m'étonne

16. N'avez-vous pas . . . d'avoir fait cette bêtise?

    (A) courage
    (B) joie
    (C) hâte
    (D) honte

17. Ce tissu est . . . comme la peau d'un bébé.

    (A) mouillé
    (B) nu
    (C) doux
    (D) cru

18. Le renard a . . . aux chasseurs.

    (A) ramassé
    (B) enfui
    (C) échappé
    (D) couru

19. Le film commence à 8 heures exactement; soyez . . .

    (A) à l'heure
    (B) au courant
    (C) au loin
    (D) à présent

20. Il y a trop de monde ici; je préfère des cafés moins . . .

    (A) doués
    (B) chargés
    (C) tranquilles
    (D) fréquentés

21. Il n'y a pas assez de preuves pour . . . cet homme. *evidence*

    (A) indiquer
    (B) inquiéter
    (C) insinuer
    (D) inculper

22. Mon frère est . . . ; il ne veut jamais m'aider à nettoyer la cuisine.

    (A) serviable
    (B) paresseux
    (C) redoutable
    (D) affolé

23. Le vase que j'ai laissé tomber s'est . . .

   (A) perdu
   (B) tricoté
   (C) évanoui
   (D) brisé

24. Vous pouvez trouver la robe de mariée de votre
    grand-mère si vous cherchez dans . . .

   (A) le plancher
   (B) le grenier
   (C) l'atelier
   (D) le magasin

25. Elle s'est débarrassée de ses vêtements . . .

   (A) âgés
   (B) déprimés
   (C) abîmés
   (D) achetés

26. Diane s'est coupé les . . . pour être plus à la mode.

   (A) chevaux
   (B) chiffres
   (C) cheveux
   (D) chemins

27. Pour établir la validité de sa théorie, l'homme de
    science a fait . . .

   (A) un échec
   (B) une expérience
   (C) un résumé
   (D) un résultat

Summary

To increase your score, keep the following tips in mind.

- o If you know all the words in the sentence
    - • eliminate obviously wrong answer choices
    - • examine remaining choices (to avoid obvious traps)
    - • pick your answer

- o If you are not sure of the meaning of the sentence
    - • use word association
    - • read the question again, and see if there are any obvious traps

- o If you do not know all of the answer choices
    - • use your English to eliminate wrong answers
    - • try to figure out the roots of the words

- o Guess after you have eliminated as many obviously wrong answers as possible.

Chapter 4
Vocabulary Review

At this level, your basic French vocabulary should be good. The more French you read, the better you will acquire new words and feel comfortable with what you already know. The following vocabulary list should help you review. It organizes words in logical categories. This will make memorizing them easier. Look through each category and concentrate on the words you don't know or words that seem to be cognates but in fact have very different meanings.

BOOST YOUR VOCABULARY

If you really want to imprint new vocabulary words on your brain, passive reading is not enough. Critical reading with a dictionary at hand, as well as listening and watching French media will increase your vocabulary significantly. Try one or more of the following techniques to help your learning.

Flashcards

Put the French word on one side, the English on the other. If you want to get fancy, color-code by category or make up a symbol. This way, you can mix up words in any order and regroup them in many different ways, such as where, when, and how the words can be used. On the French side, include part of speech, gender, and the word used in a sentence. Whenever you have a few minutes, pull out your cards and test yourself. Think of this as a game.

Mnemonics

If it works for you, think of a funny image or sound that corresponds to the word. The more outrageous, the easier it will be to remember. Make up your own mnemonics and add them to your flashcards.

Posters

Make a list of words and definitions and hang them on your wall. As you go about your day, glance at the poster and review a few words.

These are only a few of the ways you can work on your vocabulary. Anything you do to make it more creative or colorful (literally—use colored pens, colored index cards, stickers, or markers) will increase your ability to learn and remember vocabulary.

Color-code your vocabulary list! Use three different highlighters to keep track of words you know, words you sort of know, and words you've never seen before. Assign a different color to each category so you know which words you need to work on.

VOCABULARY LIST

This section will help you review key vocabulary words. It is not the only vocabulary you need to know for the test, however. You will find suggestions for how to continue enriching your vocabulary. Pay particular attention to the commonly mixed-up words and false cognates.

Le Calendrier et le Temps — The Calendar and the Time

Une Année — A Year

un an	a year (always used for age)
une décennie	a decade
une année	a year (as in *l'année dernière*, last year)
un mois	a month
une semaine	a week
un jour	a day
une journée	a day (as in *toute la journée*, all day long)
un siècle	a century
un calendrier	a calendar
un horaire	a schedule

Un Jour — A Day

le matin	the morning
la matinée	the morning
l'après-midi (m or f)	the afternoon
le soir	the evening
la soirée	the evening
la nuit	the night
l'aube (f)	daybreak
l'aurore (f)	dawn
le crépuscule	twilight
le lever du soleil	the sunrise
le coucher du soleil	the sunset
un jour férié	a holiday
un jour de congé	a day off
faire la grasse matinée	to sleep late

Une Heure — An Hour

minuit	midnight
midi	noon
une montre	a watch
un réveil	an alarm clock
une horloge, une pendule	a clock
un minuteur	a timer (in the kitchen)
un chronomètre	a stop watch

_Un An_ vs. _Une Année_
What's the difference between *un an* and *une année*? It's subtle. *Un an* is a unit of time. For example, *"J'ai passé deux ans à Paris." Une année* is used when describing not the unit, but the full span of time. For example, *"l'année que j'ai passée en France. . . ."* The same concept is used for *un matin—une matinée, un soir—une soirée, un jour—une journée.*

Lundi vs. _Le Lundi_
Observe what happens when you use the definite article *le. Lundi* means "Monday." *Le lundi* means "on Mondays." Also, notice the following expressions: *Tous les lundis* means "every Monday." *Lundi en huit* means "a week from Monday." (Monday to Monday is eight days.)

The expressions of time are very important to have memorized when choosing a tense or a mode of conjugation.

Les Expressions de Temps | Expressions of Time

être à l'heure	to be on time
être en retard	to be late
être en avance	to be ahead of schedule
tôt	early
tard	late
avant	before
après	after
le lendemain	the day after
hier	yesterday
désormais	from now on / from then on
pendant	during
arriver de bonne heure	to arrive early
déjà	already
bientôt	soon
prochainement	shortly
toujours	always / still
ne…pas encore	not yet
ne…jamais	never
longtemps	for a long time
régulièrement	regularly
d'habitude	usually
habituellement	usually
autrefois	in the past
parfois	sometimes
chaque jour	each / every day
se dépêcher	to hurry
se précipiter	to rush
Un instant!	Just a moment!
Ne quittez pas!	please hold (on)!

Au printemps means "in (the) spring." For pronunciation reasons, *en* is used in front of *hiver, été* and *automne* to translate "in." En *hiver,* en *été,* en *automne.*

Les Saisons (f) | Seasons

le printemps	spring
l'été (m)	summer
l'automne (m)	autumn, fall
l'hiver (m)	winter

La Nature et le temps	Nature and the weather
la météo	the weather forecast
le soleil	the sun, the sunshine
être bronzé	to be tanned
prendre un coup de soleil	to get sunburnt
attraper une insolation	to get sunstroke
Quel temps fait-il?	What's the weather like?
il fait beau	the weather is nice
il fait chaud	it is hot
avoir chaud	to be hot
par beau temps	in good weather
le nuage	the cloud
la pluie	the rain
il pleut / pleuvoir	it is raining / to rain
une averse	a shower
il pleut des cordes	it's raining cats and dogs
être trempé(e)	to be soaked
être mouillé(e)	to be wet
il fait mauvais	the weather is bad
par mauvais temps	in bad weather
la neige	the snow
la glace	the ice
il neige	it is snowing
il fait froid	it is cold
avoir froid	to be cold
un ciel couvert	an overcast sky
un orage	a thunderstorm
il y a des éclairs	there is lightning
le tonnerre	thunder
le brouillard	the fog
la brume	light fog / a mist
le vent	the wind
une tempête	a storm
un ouragan	a hurricane
la rosée du matin	the morning dew
une rafale de vent	a gust of wind
une bourrasque	a squall

Pleurer* vs. *Pleuvoir
A common mistake is to mix up *pleurer* (to cry) and *pleuvoir* (to rain).

briller	to shine
souffler	to blow
il fait noir / sombre	it is dark
prédire	to predict

Le Plein Air — The Outdoors

dehors	outside
un arbre	a tree
un buisson	a bush
l'écorce d'un arbre	the bark
une feuille	a leaf
une prairie	a meadow
un champ	a field
l'herbe (f)	grass
le gazon / la pelouse	the lawn
une rivière	a river
un fleuve	a river flowing into the sea
la mer	the sea
une étoile	a star
la lune	the moon
un verger	an orchard
le jardin	the garden
une fleur	a flower
la poussière	the dust
récolter	to harvest
ramasser	to gather, to pick up
se promener / faire une promenade	to take a walk
prendre l'air	to get some fresh air, to take a walk
faire une randonnée	to go hiking
tondre la pelouse	to mow the lawn

La Maison — The Home

un toit	a roof
un plafond	a ceiling
une cheminée	a chimney, a fireplace
un mur	a wall
une fenêtre	a window

un volet	a shutter
en haut	upstairs
en bas	downstairs
les toilettes / les WC	the restroom (toilet)
la salle de bains	the bathroom (bath)
une baignoire	a bathtub
prendre un bain	to take a bath
une douche	a shower
prendre une douche / se doucher	to take a shower
une serviette	a towel
un savon	a bar of soap
un lavabo	a bathroom sink
une glace / un miroir	a mirror
la chambre à coucher	the bedroom
un lit	a bed
une armoire	a closet
un meuble	a piece of furniture
un tiroir	a drawer
un aspirateur	a vacuum cleaner
un climatiseur	an air conditioner
un rideau	a curtain
un oreiller	a pillow
un matelas	a mattress
une couverture	a blanket
un drap	a sheet
un plancher	a wooden floor
le sol	the floor
le salon / la salle de séjour	the living room
une chaise	a chair
un divan / un canapé	a couch
un tableau	a painting, a picture
un fauteuil	an armchair
ouvrir	to open
fermer	to close
se coucher	to go to bed
s'endormir	to fall asleep
se réveiller	to wake up

This Should "Cover" It
Some common mix-ups are *les couvertures* (the blankets), *le couvert* (the table setting), and *le couvercle* (the lid).

s'allonger	to lie down
avoir sommeil	to be sleepy
se lever	to get up
s'asseoir	to sit down
la salle à manger	the dining room
la cuisine	the kitchen
un évier	a kitchen sink
un four	an oven
un appareil ménager	an appliance
un réfrigérateur	a refrigerator
une poubelle	a garbage can
un pot	a jar
une casserole	a pan
une poêle	a frying pan
une cuisinière	a stove
un cuisinier / une cuisinière	a cook
le grenier	the attic
la cave	the cellar
un coin	a corner
le sous-sol	the basement
un atelier	a studio, a workshop
le rez-de-chaussée	the ground floor
un / une concierge	a building superintendent / a custodian
une boîte à lettres	a mail box
le courrier	the mail
frotter	to rub
astiquer	to polish
balayer	to sweep
nettoyer	to clean
faire le ménage	to do the housework
faire la vaisselle	to wash the dishes
faire la cuisine	to cook
faire la poussière	to dust
ranger	to put away
monter	to go up / to bring up
descendre	to go down / to bring down
rester	to stay

False Cognates
Un coin means "a corner," NOT "a coin." Une pièce de monnaie is a coin. Un pot means "a jar" or "a pot." Une cave means "a cellar." Une caverne is a cave. Un plat means "a dish" (as in part of a meal). Une assiette is a plate.

quitter (+ un nom)	to leave
partir	to leave
se reposer	to rest
bricoler	to fix

En Ville (f)

In Town

un immeuble	a building
un gratte-ciel	a skyscraper
un trottoir	a sidewalk
un passant	a passer-by
une rue	a street
un rond-point	a traffic circle
une zone piétonne	a pedestrian zone
un quartier	a neighborhood
un endroit	a place
une gare	a train station
une piscine	a swimming pool
une banlieue	a suburb
habiter dans les environs de	to live on the outskirts of
habiter en banlieue	to live in the suburbs
un stade	a stadium
un théâtre	a theater
assister à un concert	to attend a concert
une foule	a crowd
la boulangerie	the bakery
un boulanger / une boulangère	a baker
une pâtisserie	a pastry shop, a pastry
un pâtissier / une pâtissière	a pastry cook
une épicerie	a grocery store
un épicier / une épicière	a grocer
une fromagerie	a cheese store
une boucherie	a butcher shop
un boucher / une bouchère	a butcher
une charcuterie	a delicatessen
un charcutier / une charcutière	a pork butcher
une papeterie	a stationery store

False Cognates

Rester means "to stay," NOT "to rest." *Se reposer* means "to rest." *Quitter* means "to leave," NOT "to quit." Use *quitter* instead of *partir* when you mean it to be more permanent. Examples: *Quitter son domicile; quitter son pays; quitter l'école. Abandonner* means "to quit."

False Cognates

Assister à means "to attend," NOT "to assist." *Il assiste au concert. Aider quelqu'un* means "to assist someone."

une librairie	a bookstore
une bibliothèque	a library
un marché aux puces	a flea market
une quincaillerie	a hardware store
le rayon bricolage	the do-it yourself department
un tabac / un bureau de tabac	a shop selling tobacco items, stamps, newspapers
une banque	a bank
un kiosque à journaux	a newsstand

Faire les Courses (f)   Shopping for Food

la nourriture	food
la recette	a recipe
le pain	bread
un croissant	a croissant
les pâtisseries (f)	pastries
une tarte	a tart
un gâteau	a cake
un chou à la crème	a cream-puff
un petit gâteau / un biscuit	a cookie
un biscuit salé	a cracker
un éclair	an éclair
les pâtes (f)	pasta
le riz	rice
le maïs	corn
les légumes (m)	vegetables
les épinards (m)	spinach
les haricots verts (m)	green beans
un oignon	an onion
un champignon	a mushroom
un poivron vert	a green pepper
les pommes de terre	potatoes
les petits pois	peas
un avocat	an avocado
les fruits (m)	fruit
une pomme	an apple

une fraise	a strawberry
une framboise	a raspberry
un ananas	a pineapple
une myrtille	a blueberry
une cerise	a cherry
une pêche	a peach
une poire	a pear
une noix	a walnut
une amande	an almond
des raisins	grapes
des raisins secs	raisins
un pamplemousse	a grapefruit
un concombre	a cucumber
le fromage	cheese
le beurre	butter
le lait	milk
une glace	an ice cream
un œuf	an egg
la viande	meat
le jambon	ham
le veau	veal
un rôti	a roast
une boulette de viande	a meatball
le sel	salt
le poivre	pepper
la confiture	jam, preserves
le sucre	sugar
l'eau	water
une bière	a beer
le vin	wine
livrer	to deliver
commander	to order
vendre	to sell
acheter	to buy
faire les courses	to go shopping, to run errands
avoir besoin de	to need
avoir envie de manger	to feel like eating

l'argent (m)	money
retirer de l'argent	to withdraw money
rendre la monnaie	to give back the change
payer comptant	to pay cash
économiser	to save money

Au Restaurant (m) — At the Restaurant

un restaurant	a restaurant
le repas	the meal
le déjeuner	lunch
le petit déjeuner	breakfast
le dîner	dinner
un plat	a dish
le service est compris	service is included
Et comme boissons?	And for drinks?
un garçon, un serveur	a waiter
une serveuse	a waitress
un pourboire	a tip
l'addition (f)	the bill, the check
le couvert	table setting; cover charge
une cuillère	a spoon
un couteau	a knife
une fourchette	a fork
une assiette	a plate
le verre	the glass
remplir	to fill
servir	to serve
se servir (de)	to use, to help oneself (with)
régler / payer l'addition	to pay the check
emporter	to take away
apporter	to bring
mettre le couvert	to set the table
débarrasser la table	to clear the table
se débarrasser de	to get rid of
fréquenter	to go to a place frequently
fréquenté	crowded, popular

mou / molle	soft
cru / crue	raw
cuit / cuite	cooked
bien cuit	well-done
à point	medium rare
saignant / saignante	rare
gras / grasse	greasy, fatty

Le Monde du Travail   The Working World

le chômage	unemployment
un(e) chômeur / chômeuse	an unemployed person
un ouvrier	a worker
la médecine du travail	occupational medicine
un médecin	a physician
un infirmier / une infirmière	a nurse
le droit	law
un(e) avocat(e)	a lawyer
un(e) juge	a judge
le monde artistique	the arts
un chanteur / une chanteuse	a singer
un acteur / une actrice	an actor, an actress
un(e) metteur en scène	a director, a producer
une œuvre	a work
un chef-d'œuvre	a masterpiece
le commerce / les affaires	business
une femme / un homme d'affaires	a business woman / man
un(e) comptable	an accountant
un(e) patron / patronne	a boss
un / une cadre	an executive
l'informatique (f)	computer science
un ordinateur	a computer
la facture	the bill, the invoice
l'usine (f)	the factory
l'outil (m)	the tool
embaucher	to hire
travailler	to work

False Cognates
Travailler means to work, not to travel

être en grève / faire grève	to be on strike
renvoyer	to dismiss
mettre à la porte	to fire
licencier	to lay off

Le Corps Humain   The Human Body

la tête	the head
la figure, le visage	the face
l'œil / les yeux (m)	the eye / the eyes
le nez	the nose
la bouche	the mouth
la lèvre	the lip
la dent	the tooth
la langue	the tongue
l'oreille (f)	the ear
le cou	the neck
l'épaule (f)	the shoulder
la poitrine	the chest
le bras	the arm
la main	the hand
le doigt	the finger
le coude	the elbow
l'ongle (m)	the nail
le poignet	the wrist
la hanche	the hip
la jambe	the leg
le genou / les genoux	the knee / knees
les cheveux	the hair
la peau	the skin
le poumon	the lung
le cœur	the heart
le ventre	the belly
le talon	the heel
le poing	the fist
un coup de poing	a punch
le rein	the kidney

l'orteil	the toe
le dos	the back
un os	a bone
le sang	the blood
transpirer, suer	to sweat
respirer	to breathe
se faire mal à l'épaule	to hurt one's shoulder
avoir mal au ventre / à l'estomac	to have a stomachache
gros	fat
mince	slim, thin
maigre	skinny
être en forme	to be in shape
décontracté(e)	relaxed
muet / muette	mute
aveugle	blind
sourd(e)	deaf
se laver	to wash (oneself)
se brosser les dents	to brush one's teeth
se peigner	to comb one's hair
se coiffer	to do one's hair
se raser	to shave
se maquiller	to put makeup on
du rouge à lèvres	a lipstick
une crème	a cream
se sécher	to dry oneself

The expression *avoir mal* should be used with the proper preposition *au, à la, à l'*, or *aux* depending on the body part following the expression. *J'ai mal à la tête; il a mal aux jambes.*

Les Vêtements (m)   Clothes

au rayon femmes / hommes	in the women's / men's department
en solde	on sale
une robe	a dress
une robe du soir	a gown
une robe de chambre	a robe
un peignoir de bain	a bathrobe
une chemise de nuit	a nightgown
un chemisier	a woman's shirt
une chemise	a shirt

un tailleur	a woman's suit
un ensemble	a woman's suit, an outfit
un costume	a man's suit
un smoking	a tuxedo, dinner jacket
une jupe	a skirt
un pull	a sweater
un col roulé	a turtleneck sweater
un manteau	a coat
un imperméable	a raincoat
un parapluie	an umbrella
une chaussure / un soulier	a shoe
une botte	a boot
une chaussette	a sock
des collants (m)	tights
un pantalon	a pair of pants
un survêtement	a sweatsuit, a warmup suit
les sous-vêtements (m. pl.)	underwear
une manche	a sleeve
un bouton	a button
une poche	a pocket
un maillot de bain	a swimming suit / a bathing suit
une ceinture	a belt
un chapeau	a hat
une casquette	a cap
un foulard	a scarf
une écharpe	a winter scarf, a sash
une cravate	a tie
un collier	a necklace
une bague	a ring
une boucle d'oreille	an earring
un fil	a thread
la soie	silk
la laine	wool
le cuir	leather
le caoutchouc	rubber
le velours côtelé	corduroy
la fourrure	fur

l'aiguille	the needle
la taille	size, waist
la pointure	shoe size
le cintre	the hanger
essayer	to try on
porter	to wear
mettre	to put on
froisser	to wrinkle
repasser	to iron
le repassage	ironing
déchirer	to tear
coudre	to sew
la couture	sewing
le tricot	knitting
tricoter	to knit
rétrécir	to shrink
aller bien	to suit / to go well
être à la bonne taille	to fit
avoir de l'allure	to have style
propre	clean
une tache	a stain
taché(e)	stained
à la mode	in style, fashionable
décontracté(e)	casual
démodé(e)	out of style
assorti(e) à	matching
uni(e)	solid color
à rayures	striped
imprimé(e)	printed
ecossais(e)	plaid
à fleurs	floral
à pois	polka-dotted
à carreaux	checked
délavé(e)	faded, washed-out

Allure means "appearance," but it also means "speed" or "pace." *Il va à toute allure!* "He is going at top speed!"

Tache vs. **Tâche**
Une tache means "a stain." *Une tâche* means "a task."

Les Voyages/ Les Transports

Travel/ Transportation

Les Voyages/ Les Transports	Travel/ Transportation
un voyage	a trip
faire un voyage	to go on a trip
faire ses valises	to pack one's suitcases
être en vacances	to be on vacation
l'itinéraire	the itinerary, the route
la route	the way / the road
un vélo, une bicyclette	a bicycle
une voiture	a car, a carriage, a wagon
une voiture d'occasion	a second-hand car
une ceinture de sécurité	a seatbelt
une autoroute	a highway
un bouchon / un embouteillage	a traffic jam
l'heure de pointe / d'affluence	rush hour / peak hour
rouler	to move forward, to roll, to drive
conduire	to drive
doubler une voiture	to pass a car
klaxonner	to honk
interdiction de stationner	no parking
tourner à gauche / à droite	turn left / right
défense de tourner à gauche	no left turn
se garer	to park
démarrer	to start driving
un permis de conduire	a driving license
l'essence	gas
faire le plein	to fill up the tank
avoir une panne d'essence	to run out of gas
une roue	a wheel
un pneu	a tire
un pneu crevé	a flat tire
un volant	a steering wheel
un frein	a brake
un rétroviseur	a rearview mirror
un phare	a headlight
une station-service	a gas station

Un bouchon also means "a cork." *Un embouteillage* comes from the word *une bouteille*, "a bottle."

s'arrêter	to stop
reculer	to back up
un train	a train
le chemin de fer	the railroad
une gare	a train station
un guichet	a ticket booth
demander un renseignement	to ask for information
composter	to punch in (tickets)
rater (le train)	to miss (the train)
une correspondance	a train connection, a transfer
le prochain arrêt	the next stop
un contrôleur	a ticket inspector
changer	to transfer
monter	to get on
descendre	to get off
un bateau	a boat
une voile	a sail
une bouée de sauvetage	a life preserver
un gilet de sauvetage	a life jacket
avoir le mal de mer	to be seasick
une croisière	a cruise
un avion	a plane
atterrir / se poser	to land
l'atterrissage	the landing
enregistrer les bagages	to check in (one's luggage)
décoller	to take off
le décollage	takeoff
une escale	a stop, a stopover
une aile	a wing
avoir le mal de l'air	to feel airsick
voler	to fly
un vol	a flight
l'embarquement	boarding
la douane	customs
un billet	a ticket
un aller simple	a one-way ticket
un aller-retour	a roundtrip ticket

une agence de voyages	a travel agency
traverser	to cross
transporter	to transport
proche	near
loin	far
le décalage horaire	the time difference, jet lag
une fusée	a rocket
complet	full
il y a de la place	there is room
une place libre	an empty seat
annulé(e)	cancelled

Les Accidents et les Urgences

Accidents and Emergencies

le dégât	the damage
la faute	the mistake, the fault
grave	serious
le témoin	the witness
une blessure	an injury
une brûlure	a burn
l'assurance (f)	the insurance
la prison	the jail
un incendie	a wildfire, a fire
un feu	a fire
une piqûre d'insecte	a sting / an insect bite
enfermer	to lock up
se couper	to cut oneself
brûler	to burn
saigner	to bleed
se casser (la jambe)	to break (one's leg)
être témoin de	to witness
assurer	to ensure, to assure
arrêter	to stop, to arrest
renverser quelqu'un	to hit somebody (with a vehicle)
soutenir	to hold up, to support
secourir, aider	to help to save / to rescue

Aidez-moi!
You call for help in French by yelling *"Au secours!"*

avoir tort	to be wrong
avoir raison	to be right
échapper à	to escape (from)
attraper	to catch
éviter	to avoid
blesser	to injure
assommer	to knock out (a person)
faire tomber	to knock down (something)
tomber	to fall
glisser	to slip
faire un plâtre / plâtrer	to put a cast on
faire un pansement	to put a bandage / a dressing on
s'étrangler	to choke
la réanimation	resuscitation
sortir indemne	to come out unharmed
heureusement	fortunately
malheureusement	unfortunately

False Cognates
Blesser means "to hurt;" *se blesser* means "to get hurt," NOT "to bless." *Sauver* means "to save" or "to rescue." If you mean "to save money," you must use the word *économiser*, and *se sauver* means "to run away."

La Maladie — Illness

un rhume	a cold
une angine	a throat infection
des vertiges	dizzy spells
la nausée	nausea
une crampe	a cramp
la douleur	pain
une baisse de tension	a drop in blood pressure
la rougeole	measles
la varicelle	chicken pox
la chirurgie	surgery
la salle d'attente	the waiting room
un rendez-vous	an appointment
une ordonnance	a prescription
un comprimé	a pill
un cachet	a tablet
prendre des médicaments	to take medicines or medication
une analyse de sang	a blood test

avaler	to swallow
avoir mal au cœur	to feel nauseated
avoir des boutons	to have a rash
être enrhumé(e)	to have a cold
avoir de la fièvre	to have a fever
avoir la grippe	to have the flu
avoir de la tension	to have high blood pressure
avoir des palpitations	to have palpitations
s'évanouir	to faint
vomir	to throw up
éternuer	to sneeze
tousser	to cough
avoir mal à la gorge	to have a sore throat
avoir mal à la tête	to have a headache
le traitement	the treatment
soigner	to treat
se soigner	to take care of oneself
vacciner contre	to vaccinate against
faire une piqûre	to give a shot
faire une radio	to take an X-ray
aller / se porter bien...mal / mieux	to be well / ill / better
être en bonne santé / bien portant	to be in good health
être en pleine forme	to be in top shape
déprimé(e)	depressed
malade	sick, ill

L'émotion (f)   Emotion

la confiance	confidence or trust
le plaisir	pleasure
la hâte	haste
la honte	shame
la méfiance	mistrust
l'agrément (m)	pleasure; approval
un caprice	a whim
une larme	a tear
un baiser	a kiss
combler (quelqu'un)	to gratify / to satisfy
être d'accord	to agree
s'occuper (de)	to take care of
éprouver	to feel, to experience
étonner	to astonish
s'étonner de	to be amazed by
estimer	to hold in esteem; to estimate
tolérer	to tolerate
surprendre	to surprise
se méfier (de)	to distrust
faire de la peine (à)	to hurt someone's feelings
avoir de la peine	to feel bad
tromper	to trick, to deceive
se tromper	to make a mistake
changer d'avis	to change one's mind
s'amuser	to have fun
rire	to laugh
sourire	to smile
pleurer	to cry
s'embêter / s'ennuyer	to be bored
s'énerver	to get upset

Avoir and Emotions

Many expressions with *avoir* describe an emotion:

avoir confiance (en)	to trust
avoir peur (de)	to be afraid
avoir honte (de)	to be ashamed of
avoir de la peine	to be sad
avoir hâte (de)	to be eager to, to be impatient to

"Félicitations!"

You congratulate someone in French by saying *"Félicitations!"* or *"Je te félicite!"*

The verb *manquer* has a few meanings:

Tu me manques, or *vous me manquez.*	I miss you.
Il a manqué le train et son rendez-vous.	He missed the train and his appointment.
Elle a manqué son gateau.	She ruined her cake.

False Cognate

Crier means "to shout," NOT "to cry."

A great idiom (very colloquial) for expressing frustration is *J'en ai ras-le-bol!* which means roughly, "I've had it up to here!"

jurer	to swear
j'en ai marre / j'en ai assez	I am fed up, I have had enough
taquiner	to tease
se quereller	to quarrel
se disputer	to have an argument / to argue
se réconcilier avec	to make up with
se réjouir de	to look forward
prévoir	to predict
se souvenir de	to remember
soutenir	to give support
rompre (avec)	to break up (with)
se fâcher (avec)	to get upset (at)
se douter de quelque chose	to suspect something
sembler	to seem
craindre	to fear, to be afraid of

menacer	to threaten
avoir le coup de foudre pour	to fall in love at first sight
tomber amoureux de	to fall in love (with)
s'entendre	to get along
plaindre	to feel sorry for
en vouloir à	to be angry at, to have a grudge against
Ne t'en fais pas!	Don't worry!
Ça va s'arranger!	It's going to get better!
profiter de	to take advantage of
convaincre	to convince
ennuyeux / ennuyeuse	boring
ennuyé(e)	bored, embarrassed, in trouble
joyeux / joyeuse	joyful
heureux / heureuse	happy
content(e)	glad, pleased, happy, content
de bonne humeur	in a good mood
de mauvaise humeur	in a bad mood

It Seems to Me…

Avoir l'air means "to appear" or "to look."

Elle a l'air fatigue.

> She looks tired.

Sentir means "to smell" (having an odor or noticing an odor).

Elle sent quelque chose de bon dans le four.

> She can smell something nice in the oven.

Ce poulet sent bon.

> This chicken smells good.

Se sentir means "to feel."

Comment te sens-tu aujourd'hui?

> How do you feel today?

Je me sens seul.

> I feel lonely.

Ressentir (+ noun) means "to feel" (a pain or an emotion).

triste	sad
fier / fière	proud
énervé(e)	edgy
énervant(e)	irritating
comblé(e)	fortunate, happy
méchant(e)	mean, nasty
bassement	meanly, nastily
malheureux / malheureuse	unhappy
savant(e)	learned, knowledgeable
en colère, fâché(e)	angry
honteux / honteuse	shameful, ashamed
sage	wise
profond(e)	profound or deep
inquiet / inquiète	worried
préoccupé(e)	worried
déçu(e)	disappointed
tendu(e)	uptight, tense
ravi(e)	delighted
étonné(e)	astonished
ému(e)	moved, touched
fou / folle	crazy
dévoué(e) à	devoted to
exquis(e)	exquisite
bouleversé(e)	overwhelmed
vaniteux / vaniteuse	vain

If you want to tell someone to be happy, good, proud, etc., use the imperative of the verb *être* + an adjective.
Soyez sages! Be good!
Sois confiant! Have faith! or Be confident!
Sois fier! Be proud!
Sois content! Be happy!

Work on your memorization: Regroup the verbs, nouns, and adjectives that carry the same meaning. Example: *la dévotion; se dévouer; dévoué.*

Les Expressions de Quantité

Expressions of Quantity

le numéro	number
le nombre	number (as in quantity)
le compte	count, account
la somme	sum
les chiffres	figures, numerals, digits
évaluer	to evaluate
l'augmentation (f)	increase / raise
la croissance	growth

la subvention	the subsidy
le manque	lack
rien	nothing
tout	everything
tout le monde	everybody
beaucoup de	a lot of, many
un peu de	a little of, a few
peu de	little / few
trop de	too many, too much
moins de	fewer, less than
quelques	some, a few
aucun / aucune	none, not any
un tas de	a stack of, many
plein de	full of
le taux	the rate
les frais (m,pl.)	expenses, costs

The French school system is quite different from that of the U.S. By high school (*le lycée*), students have been divided into categories, each of which has a learning specialty: sciences, languages, economics, literature, etc. At the end of *le lycée*, students must pass a comprehensive exam in their specialty, *le baccalauréat (le bac)*, to graduate.

L'école (f)   School

une bourse d'études	a scholarship
une sortie scolaire	a field trip
une moyenne	a grade point average
un carnet de notes	a report card (elementary school)
un bulletin scolaire	a report card (secondary school)
une interrogation	a quiz, a test
un dossier	a file
un débouché	a career prospect
une agrafeuse	a stapler
la colle	glue
un rapporteur	a protractor
un panneau d'affichage	a bulletin board
une bonne note	a good grade
une erreur	a mistake
feuilleter	to leaf through
permettre	to permit, to allow
traduire	to translate
écrire	to write

enseigner	to teach
parler couramment	to speak fluently
une dissertation	an essay, a paper
admettre	to admit
noter	to grade
suivre / prendre des cours	to take classes
souligner	to underline
faire une erreur / se tromper	to make a mistake
corriger	to correct
constater une erreur	to notice a mistake
passer un examen	to take an exam
rater	to flunk / to fail
sécher sur un sujet	to draw a blank in
sécher un cours	to skip a class
échouer à	to fail
être reçu(e) à un examen	to pass an exam
coller un(e) élève	to give a detention to a student
recaler	to fail a student
être recalé(e) à un examen	to fail a test
doué(e)	gifted
futé(e)	smart
perturbateur / perturbatrice	disruptive

False Cognate
Passer un examen means "to take an exam," NOT "to pass an exam."

Les Sports (m)

Sports

l'escrime	fencing
l'équitation	horseback riding
la natation	swimming
le parapente	parasailing
l'entraînement	practice, training
le vestiaire	a locker room
un but	a goal
la course	a race
le filet	the net
le cerceau	the hoop
une piste	a trail, a track, a rink, a floor
un terrain	a ground, a pitch, a field, a course

un sifflet	a whistle
un arbitre	a referee, an umpire
une médaille	a medal
un exploit	a feat
le football	soccer
la Coupe du Monde	the World Cup
le poids	weight
tenter	to attempt, to tempt
atteindre	to reach
étendre le bras	to stretch out one's arm
entraîner	to train, to coach
s'entraîner	to practice, to train
attraper	to catch
lancer	to throw
accomplir	to achieve
sauter	to jump
s'assouplir	to limber up, to become supple
repousser	to push back
monter	to go up
escalader, grimper	to climb
être ex aequo / faire match nul	to tie
souple	flexible
vif / vive	quick, lively
un coup déloyal(e)	a foul

Les Faux Amis		Common Mix-Ups		
la librairie	bookstore	**and**	*la bibliothèque*	the library
la gare	the train station	**and**	*la station service*	the gas station
le billet	the ticket	**and**	*la facture*	the bill
décevoir	to disappoint	**and**	*tromper*	to deceive
crier	to shout, to scream	**and**	*pleurer*	to cry
une course	an errand	**and**	*un cours* *une classe*	a class, a course of study
une course	a race	**and**	*la race*	the race, the ethnicity
le couvert	the table setting, the cover charge	**and**	*la couverture*	the cover, the blanket
blesser	to wound, to hurt	**and**	*bénir*	to bless
l'éditeur	the publisher	**and**	*le rédacteur*	the editor
le spectacle	the show, the play	**and**	*les lunettes*	the eyeglasses
l'agrément	the pleasure, the approval	**and**	*l'accord*	the agreement
le stage	the training course, the internship	**and**	*la scène*	the stage
la droguerie	hardware store	**and**	*la pharmacie*	drugstore
la location	the rental	**and**	*le lieu/l'éndroit*	the location
passer un examen	to take an exam	**and**	*réussir un examen*	to pass an exam

Only two or three questions on Part A will have tricky mix-ups.

Vocabulary questions on Part C will often have mix-ups. Usually you will be given four words that are close in meaning or look alike.

French words that look and sound similar but have different meanings			
pleurer	to cry	*pleuvoir*	to rain
tromper	to deceive	*tremper*	to soak
vouloir	to want	*en vouloir à*	to be angry at
douter	to doubt	*se douter de*	to suspect

Summary

Review the categories of vocabulary and use the study technique that works best for you.

- *Le calendrier et le temps*

- *Les expressions de temps*

- *La nature*

- *Le plein air*

- *La maison*

- *En ville*

- *Faire les courses*

- *Au restaurant*

- *Le monde du travail*

- *Le corps humain*

- *Les vêtements*

- *Les voyages / Les transports*

- *Les accidents et les urgences*

- *La maladie*

- *L'émotion*

- *Les expressions de quantité*

- *L'école*

- *Les sports*

Chapter 5
Grammar Review

Grammar is tested in Parts B and C of the SAT French Subject Test. Part B tests only grammar, while Part C tests both grammar and vocabulary. The same points of grammar are tested in Parts B and C. The SAT French Subject Test contains questions about very specific aspects of French grammar. Therefore, it is one of the easiest sections on which to improve. If you can remember and master a few rules, you'll easily get more points. This chapter will explain exactly what you need to know. First, look at the point-by-point summary of the question types you can expect. Then, keep the question style in mind as you review your French grammar. Not all that you have learned in school will be included in the test, but you may find it helpful to go back to your textbooks for more examples on the topics we suggest. We focus on the grammatical topics and difficulties most often encountered on the SAT: pronouns, verbs, prepositions, and adverbs.

PART B: GRAMMAR

Part B will consist of approximately 15 to 20 questions, placed in order of difficulty. The first third of the questions will be easy, the next third will be of intermediate difficulty, and the final third will be the most challenging.

In these questions, there will be a sentence with a blank. You will choose the answer that is grammatically correct.

Become familiar with these directions that appear on the real test:

Part B

Directions: Each of the following sentences contains a blank. From the four choices given, select the one that can be inserted in the blank to form a grammatically correct sentence and fill in the corresponding oval on the answer sheet. Choice (A) may consist of dashes that indicate that no insertion is required to form a grammatically correct sentence.

Jean-Claude est venu avec -------.

(A) ils = eux
(B) leur
(C) eux
(D) soi

The correct answer is (C).

PART C: COMPLETE THE PARAGRAPH

Part C tests both grammar and vocabulary.

Part C tests both grammar and vocabulary. In this section, there are approximately 12 to 20 questions in no clear order of difficulty.

On this part of the test, several questions are combined in one paragraph. You may have three or four mini-paragraphs with three to five blanks within each, or you may have one long paragraph. You are asked to select the answers that best complete the sentences on the basis of either vocabulary or grammar.

Become familiar with these directions:

Part C

Directions: The paragraphs below contain blank spaces indicating omissions in the text. For some blanks, it is necessary to choose the completion that is most appropriate to the meaning of the passage; for other blanks, to choose the one completion that forms a grammatically correct sentence. In some instances, choice (A) may consist of dashes that indicate that no insertion is required to form a grammatically correct sentence. In each case, indicate your answer by filling in the corresponding oval on the answer sheet. Be sure to read each paragraph completely before answering the questions related to it.

This section combines the characteristics of Parts A and B. The small differences between the two are discussed at the end of this chapter.

KNOW WHAT YOU ARE LOOKING FOR

All the grammar questions on the SAT French Subject Test will fall into one of the following four categories.

1. Pronouns
2. Verbs
3. Prepositions
4. Odds and ends

The best way to improve in these areas is to learn the grammatical rules that are tested again and again. These rules are covered in the following grammar review.

GRAMMAR REVIEW

Grammar is a great area to focus your attention for this test. Why? Because to do well on the grammar review you need to review only a limited number of rules. Those rules will lead you to the right answer again and again. Unlike vocabulary, where luck determines whether the words you've learned will show up, grammar rules—and therefore, the content of these test questions—stay the same.

You'll be tested primarily on three things: pronouns, verbs, and prepositions. Each

Good News
Only a minuscule number of grammar questions (around two) will test you on whether a noun is masculine or feminine.

question will address only one grammatical point. We'll cover each of these categories, giving you the rules that get you right answers. We'll also give practice questions for each category. Finally, we'll cover some odds and ends that occasionally show up on the test.

BASIC TERMS

You won't be tested on this material, but take a quick look through to make sure that you understand what the following terms mean. We'll be using them in this grammar review.

Parts of Speech

1. **Noun**—a person, place, thing, quality, or action. It can be either a subject or an object
2. **Verb**—the action that is being performed by the subject
3. **Pronoun**—a word that takes the place of a noun
4. **Preposition**—a word that expresses the relationship of one word to another in terms of direction, motion, or position
5. **Adjective**—a descriptive word that gives more information about a noun
6. **Adverb**—a word that modifies a verb, an adjective, or another adverb
7. **Article**—a small word that gives a little information about a noun

None of this terminology is needed for the test. Understanding these terms will help you comprehend the explanations in the grammar review that follows.

Sentence Structure

1. **Subject**—the person or thing in the sentence that is performing the action
2. **Compound subject**—two nouns or pronouns performing the action together
3. **Object**—the person or thing that is on the receiving end of the action
4. **Direct object**—an object that doesn't need a preposition to be the object
5. **Indirect object**—an object that needs a preposition in order to serve as the object
6. **Infinitive**—the form of a verb that uses "to," as in "to go" or "to speak"
7. **Auxiliary verb**—a helper verb, either *avoir* or *être,* that loses its own meaning to help form the compound past tense for other verbs, such as the *passé composé*. It is followed by the past participle of the conjugated verb.

8. **Semi-auxiliary verb**—a verb, such as *aller* or *venir*, that helps express a different aspect of the verbal action, such as the near future or the recent past.

9. **Past participle**—in the past tense, the form of the verb that teams up with the auxiliary or "helper" verb

Joe and Ellen	have worked	hard	for	their	promotions.
compound subject	aux. verb + past participle	adverb	preposition	possessive adjective	indirect object

They	baked	a	delicious	cake.	
subject pronoun	verb	article	adjective	direct object	

PRONOUNS

A quarter of all grammar questions on the SAT French test will challenge your knowledge of pronouns. Unlike English, which uses mainly two basic forms of pronouns (he and him, for example), French uses four important forms of pronouns: subject pronouns, direct object pronouns, indirect object pronouns, and stressed pronouns.

What Is a Pronoun?

A pronoun takes the place of a noun. It stands in for the full name or description of a person, place, or thing. In French, a pronoun will take different forms depending on what type of noun it replaces. Half of the pronoun questions on the test ask you to choose among subject pronouns, direct or indirect object pronouns, and stressed pronouns.

1. Subject Pronouns

Subject pronouns replace the subject of the sentence.

Jean a montré son dessin à Edith.
    Jean showed his drawing to Edith.

Il a montré son dessin à Edith.
    He showed his drawing to Edith.

je or *j'*	=	I	*nous*	=	we
tu	=	you	*vous*	=	you (plural or formal singular)
il	=	he	*ils*	=	they (masculine)
elle	=	she	*elles*	=	they (feminine)

The subject pronouns *il, ils, elle,* and *elles* are used for objects and people. *Il* signifies "he" or "it." *Elle* signifies "she" or "it." The subject pronoun *il* can be neutral or impersonal: *il est sept heures, il pleut, il faut que…* The subject pronoun *ils* is used for a group of males and for mixed groups, even if there are more females than males.

These pronouns are usually the wrong answer choices. Why? Because these are the pronouns with which everyone is most familiar and comfortable.

2. Direct Object Pronouns

These pronouns replace the direct object of a sentence. The direct object answers the question "what?"

> *Jean a montré **son dessin** à Edith.*
> Jean showed **his drawing** to Edith.

> *Jean **l'a** montré à Edith.*
> Jean showed **it** (the drawing) to Edith.

Notice that the direct object pronoun is placed before the verb.

When a direct object pronoun comes before a verb that starts with a vowel, the vowel in the pronoun is dropped and replaced with an apostrophe. For example, **me** becomes **m'** and **le** or **la** becomes **l'**.

me or *m'*	=	me	*nous*	=	us
te or *t'*	=	you	*vous*	=	you (plural or formal)
le or *l'*	=	him or it	*les*	=	them (person or thing both masculine and feminine)
la or *l'*	=	her or it			

3. Indirect Object Pronouns

These pronouns replace the indirect object of a sentence. The indirect object answers the questions "to what?" or "to whom?" Notice that the pronoun replaces both the indirect object and the preposition that goes with it.

Notice that the indirect object pronoun is placed before the verb.

> *Jean a montré son dessin **à Edith**.*
> Jean showed his drawing **to Edith**.

> *Jean **lui** a montré son dessin.*
> Jean showed **her** his drawing.

me or *m'*	=	me	*nous*	=	us
te or *t'*	=	you	*vous*	=	you (plural or formal)
lui	=	him or her	*leur*	=	them

Review the list of verbs that take the prepositions *de* or *à* or both, and their meaning. Some of them are listed on page 105 of this book.

Pay particular attention to the following verbs:

The verbs *écouter* (to listen to), *regarder* (to look at), and *attendre* (to wait for) are verbs that take a **direct object** in French.

The verbs *téléphoner à* (to call on the phone), *répondre à* (to answer), *demander à* (to ask), and *rendre visite à* (to visit someone), take an **indirect object** in French, but not in English.

The direct and indirect object pronouns are placed before the verb even when you use the negative form.

> *Je ne te donne pas mon nouveau pull.*
> I will not give you my new sweater.

> *Il ne leur parle pas.*
> He does not speak to them.

Note that the only differences between direct and indirect object pronouns occur in the third person singular and plural forms: *le/la/l'* vs. *lui* and *les* vs. *leur*. You are more likely to be tested on these, as you have to know the rules in order to figure out which pronoun is correct.

4. Stressed Pronouns

Stressed pronouns are used only to replace nouns representing people or animals.

moi	=	me or I	*nous*	=	us or we
toï	=	you	*vous*	=	you (plural or formal)
lui	=	him or he	*eux*	=	them or they (masculine or including both masculine and feminine)
elle	=	her or she	*elles*	=	them or they (feminine)

Uses of the Stressed Pronoun

A. After a preposition such as *à, pour, avec, chez, sans...*

Elle pense à sa soeur. Elle pense à elle.
> She thinks of **her sister**. She thinks of **her**.

Je travaille pour mes patrons. Je travaille pour eux.
> I work for **my bosses**. I work for **them**.

Je vis avec mon père. Je vis avec lui.
> I live with **my father**. I live with **him**.

Tu vas au cinéma sans ton frère. Tu vas au cinéma sans lui.
> You go to the movies without **your brother**. You go to the movies without **him**.

Tu peux rester chez mes tantes. Tu peux rester chez elles.
> You can stay at **my aunts'** house. You can stay at **their** house.

B. To reinforce a subject pronoun. There is no real English equivalent.

Moi, je parle très bien le français.
> I speak French very well.

Vous, vous êtes parfait!
> You are perfect!

C. After the expressions *c'est* and *ce n'est pas* and, of course, their various conjugated forms.

C'est ton frère qui est avec cette fille? Non, ce n'est pas lui.
> Is it **your brother** who is with this girl? No, it is not (**he**).

D. Before and after *et* and *ou* (or).

Toi et lui, vous allez bien vous amuser.
> **You** and **he** are going to have fun.

E. In short sentences with no verb.

Qui a demandé un chocolat? C'est moi.
> Who asked for a chocolate? **Me**. (I did.)

5. Interrogative Pronouns

The interrogative pronoun *lequel* (which one) is used sometimes to replace *quel* + noun.

> *Quel livre préfères-tu?*
>> **Which book** do you prefer?

> *Lequel préfères-tu?*
>> **Which one** do you prefer?

It agrees in gender and number with the noun it replaces: *lequel, laquelle, lesquels, lesquelles.*

See the table below for the use of these pronouns with prepositions *à* and *de:*

> *à + laquelle = à laquelle*　　　　*de + laquelle = de laquelle*
>
> *à + lequel = auquel*　　　　　　　*de + lequel = duquel*
>
> *à + lesquels = auxquels*　　　　　*de + lesquels = desquels*
>
> *à + lesquelles = auxquelles*　　　*de + lesquelles = desquelles*

> *J'ai deux frères. **Duquel** me parles-tu? (= de quel frère?)*
>> I have two brothers. **Which one** are you talking about?

> *Il y a plusieurs classes à choisir pour ce niveau. **Auxquelles** voulez-vous participer? (= à quelles classes?)*
>> There are several classes to choose from at this level. **Which ones** do you want to attend?

6. Demonstrative Pronouns

The demonstrative pronoun *celui* (this / the one) is used instead of *ce* + noun or *le* + noun.

It agrees in gender and number with the noun it replaces: *celui, celle, ceux, celles.*

There are a few combinations to keep in mind:

a. In a composed form
   celui-ci, celui-là, ceux-ci, celles-ci, celle-là...
   *Voilà les robes blanches. Ce sont **celles**-ci que j'aime.*
   Here are the white dresses. **These** are the ones I like.

b. With the preposition *de*
   *Ce ne sont pas mes sandales. Ce sont **celles** de Sophie.*
   These are not my sandals. **These** are Sophie's.

c. With *qui, que,* or *dont.* (See the use of these pronouns in the next section.)
   *J'aime les robes blanches, surtout **celles** qui sont à la mode.*
   I like white dresses, especially the trendy **ones**.

d. *Ce* is the neutral simple form and is used with the verb *être.*
   C'est toujours bon de se revoir!
   It's always nice to see each other again.

e. *Ceci* and *cela* are the compound neutral forms.
   Cela me donne une idée.
   This gives me an idea.

7. Reflexive Pronouns

The reflexive pronoun shows that the action is being performed both by and to the subject. Only certain verbs have reflexive forms. Most often reflexives will show up as incorrect answer choices.

Reflexive pronouns are used in French in situations in which they are not used in English. For example, *Je me lave les mains* (I wash my hands).

Tu te laves.
   You wash yourself.

Tu te laves les mains.
   You wash your hands.

me	myself	*nous*	ourselves
te	yourself	*vous*	yourselves or yourself (formal)
se	himself/herself	*se*	themselves

You might also see *moi-même, toi-même, lui-même/elle-même, soi-même* (oneself), *nous-mêmes, vous-même(s), eux-mêmes / elles-mêmes.* They would be used as stressed pronouns would be.

*Tu te coupes **toi-même** les cheveux!*
   You cut your hair **yourself**!

All reflexive verbs take the auxiliary *être* in the compound tenses. If the verb has no object, the past participle always agrees with the subject:

Elles se sont dépêchées.	They hurried.
Elle s'est coupée.	She cut herself.

However, there is no agreement in the sentence when the body part, or direct object, comes after the reflexive verb. We'll talk more about this later in the review.

Elles se sont lavé les mains.	They washed their hands.

Pronoun Summary

The following are the pronouns you should know. **You're most likely to be tested on third person singular and plural,** since these are the forms that change the most.

Subjects	Objects		Reflexive	Stressed
	Direct	Indirect		
je	*me (m')*	*me (m')*	*me (m')*	*moi*
tu	*te (t')*	*te (t')*	*te (t')*	*toi*
il, elle	*le, la (l')*	*lui*	*se, (s')*	*lui, elle*
nous	*nous*	*nous*	*nous*	*nous*
vous	*vous*	*vous*	*vous*	*vous*
ils, elles	*les*	*leur*	*se (s')*	*eux, elles*

Once you recognize each of these four main types of pronouns, you will find it easy to use Process of Elimination on the answer choices.

Because this is a multiple-choice test, you will be asked which of four pronouns go into the blank. Notice that some pronouns are always the same: *nous* and *vous.*

nous or *vous* can be:	subject
	direct object
	indirect object
	stressed
	reflexive
lui can be:	indirect object
	stressed

Pronoun Order

If the sentence contains both a direct and an indirect pronoun, always put the direct object pronoun before the indirect object pronoun.

Always use the order below.

Direct Object	before	Indirect Object
le		*lui*
la	before	
les		*leur*

*Tu donnes le cadeau à ta sœur. Tu **le lui** donnes maintenant.*
>   You give the present to your sister. You give **it to her** now.

*Tu écris cette lettre à ton frère. Oui, je **la lui** écris.*
>   You write a letter to your brother. Yes, I write **it to him**.

Indirect Object	before	Direct Object
me		*le*
te		*la*
nous	before	*les*
vous		*l'*

*Je vous prête mes livres. Je **vous les** prête.*
>   I lend my books to you. I lend **them to you**.

Pronoun Order with Commands

In negative commands, the order of pronouns follows the same rule:

*Ne **le lui** rends pas!*
>   Don't give **it** back **to him**!

*Ne **me les** donne pas!*
>   Don't give **them to me**!

In affirmative commands, the *me* becomes *moi*, and the direct or indirect pronoun (*moi, nous...*) is placed after the verb.

*Appelle-**moi** ce soir!*
>   Call **me** tonight.

*Répondez-**nous** tout de suite.*
>   Give **us** an answer right away.

When the command contains a direct pronoun and an indirect pronoun, both pronouns come after the verb. Follow the order below:

Direct Object	before	Indirect Object
le		*moi*
la	before	*lui*
les		*leur*
		nous

*Donne-**les-moi**!*
>   Give **them to me**!

*Rends-**le-lui**!*
>   Give **it** back **to her**!

Pronouns *y* and *en*

These are adverbial pronouns. Remember that *y* comes before *en*.

*Il **y** a beaucoup de fraises au marché ce matin. Il **y en** a beaucoup.*
>   **There** are lots of strawberries at the market this morning. **There** are lots **of them**.

*Il rend visite à sa tante à l'hôpital. Il **lui y** rend visite tous les jours.*
>   He visits his aunt at the hospital. He visits **her there** every day.

*Nous rencontrons souvent nos amis au cinéma. Nous **les y** rencontrons souvent*
>   We often meet our friends at the movies. We meet **them there** often.

*Tu **m'y** retrouves à six heures.*
>   You meet **me there** at six o'clock.

These pronouns are often seen in negative and affirmative commands:

*Achète-**lui-en**!*
>   Buy **him/her some**!

*Ne **leur en** prête pas!*
>   Don't lend **them any**!

*Occupe-**t'en** tout de suite!*
>   [**You**] Take care **of it** right away!

Let's practice our pronoun skills.

---○---

Paul voulait ------- faire peur.

(A) elle
(B) la
(C) lui
(D) les

Here's How to Crack It

Does the missing pronoun here serve as a subject or object? It serves as an object, so we can eliminate (A). *Elle* serves only as a subject pronoun or a stressed pronoun. We won't use a stressed pronoun because a preposition is not being used.

Does the verb *faire peur* take a direct or indirect object? Indirect. In English, "to frighten someone" takes a direct object, but in French the expression is *faire peur* à *quelqu'un*.

Often, three choices will refer to one person, the fourth to more than one person. In most cases, the one that is different will be wrong.

Let's cross out (D) *les,* which is a direct object pronoun as well as the only plural pronoun.

So, which choice is an indirect object pronoun?

Lui, (C), is the indirect pronoun for third person singular. It is the right answer. *La,* (B), is the direct object pronoun.

---○---

---○---

Je suis allé au concert sans -------.

(A) leur
(B) tu
(C) le
(D) eux

Here's How to Crack It

What type of pronoun would come after *sans*? A stressed pronoun comes after a preposition. Which of the answer choices is a stressed pronoun? Only (D). *Eux* is the stressed pronoun meaning "them." (A) is an indirect object pronoun. (B) is a subject pronoun. (C) is a direct object pronoun. (D) is the correct answer: *Je suis allé au concert sans eux.*

More Types of Pronouns

You also want to be familiar with some other types of pronouns that may show up. The following are most likely to appear on the real test as incorrect answer choices.

Possessive Pronouns

Possessive pronouns agree in gender and number with the noun that they replace.

Ce livre est à Nathalie.	*C'est le sien.*
This book is Nathalie's.	It is hers.
	(use of possessive pronoun)
Cette montre est à Pierre.	*C'est la sienne.*
This watch is Pierre's.	It is his.

Singular Pronouns

le mien / la mienne	*le nôtre / la nôtre*
le tien / la tienne	*le vôtre / la vôtre*
le sien / la sienne	*le leur / la leur*
Ce livre est à toi.	*C'est le tien.*
This book is yours.	It is yours.

Plural pronouns

les miens / les miennes	*les nôtres*
les tiens / les tiennes	*les vôtres*
les siens / les siennes	*les leurs*
Ces chaussures sont à elles.	*Ce sont les leurs.*
These shoes are theirs.	They are theirs.

Possessive pronouns must always be used with an article (*le, la, les*).

Person	Singular		Plural	
	Masc.	Fem.	Masc.	Fem.
je	*le mien*	*la mienne*	*les miens*	*les miennes*
tu	*le tien*	*la tienne*	*les tiens*	*les tiennes*
il, elle	*le sien*	*la sienne*	*les siens*	*les siennes*
nous	*le nôtre*	*la nôtre*	*les nôtres**	
vous	*le vôtre*	*la vôtre*	*les vôtres**	
ils, elles	*le leur*	*la leur*	*les leurs**	

*These represent both the masculine and the feminine forms.

Still More Types of Pronouns

About half of the pronoun questions revolve around the use of other types of pronouns (adverbial pronouns, demonstrative pronouns, relative pronouns, indefinite pronouns, etc.). Don't worry—you don't need to know the terminology.

Example:

Je n'ai pas le temps de faire les courses -------
ma mère m'a demandé de faire.

(A) qui
(B) que
(C) dont
(D) lesquelles

Which pronoun is correct?

Let's take a look at each in turn and see what rules govern their use.

Qui—Who or Which or That

Qui is the equivalent of the English "who," except that *qui* can also be used to refer to things ("that"). The *qui* **refers to the subject of the phrase.**

*la dame **qui** danse là-bas* . . .
    the lady **who** is dancing over there . . .

*la table **qui** est cassée* . . .
    the table **that** is broken . . .

Qui can also be used with a preposition. In this case, it can only refer to a person.

*l'homme sans **qui** je n'aurais rien accompli* . . .
    the man without **whom** I would have accomplished nothing . . .

Qui **vs.** *Que*
Don't use your ear to determine if **qui** or **que** is right. Learn a few rules that will help you choose: 1. Is the noun before the blank the subject or object of the phrase? 2. Is there a preposition involved?

Ce qui—What

Ce qui is used as the subject of the sentence.

> *Qu'est-ce qui se passe?*
>> **What** is happening?

> *Je ne sais pas ce qui la fait pleurer!*
>> I do not know **what**'s making her cry!

Que—Whom or That

Que is used in a number of ways in the French language. On the SAT French Test, however, it usually shows up as a relative pronoun. Roughly the equivalent of the English "whom," it refers to the person or thing that is **the object** of the action. *Que* **is never used with a preposition.**

> *l'enfant que j'ai puni . . .*
> (i.e., *j'ai puni l'enfant*)
>> the child **whom** I punished . . .

> *la bicyclette que j'ai reçue pour mon anniversaire . . .*
> (i.e., *j'ai reçu la bicyclette pour mon anniversaire*)
>> the bicycle **that** I received for my birthday . . .

Ce que—What

Ce que is used as a direct object in a sentence.

> *Je ne comprends pas ce qu'il dit.*
>> I do not understand **what** he is saying.

> *Je préfère ce que tu viens d'acheter.*
>> I prefer **what** you have just bought.

When Do You Use *Qui* and When Do You Use *Que*?

Unless there is a preposition involved, this is similar to the English use of "who" or "whom." In English, one test is to see if the "who" or "whom" would be replaced by "he" or "him," and see which sounds right:

the man _____ is smoking over there . . .
> "He" is smoking, so you would use "who."

the man _____ I hugged . . .
> I hugged "him," so you would use "whom."

If you understand "who/whom" in English, you may want to translate and decide if "who" or "whom" is correct. If "who" is correct, use *qui*; if "whom" is correct, use *que*.

> *l'homme qui fume là-bas . . .*
>> the man **who** is smoking over there . . .

> *l'homme que j'ai embrassé . . .*
>> the man **whom** I hugged . . .

What If a Preposition Is Involved?

If a preposition is involved and the pronoun refers to a person, use *qui* or the correct form of *lequel*.

> *l'homme à qui j'ai donné de l'argent . . .*
>> the man **to whom** I gave money . . .

> *l'ami pour lequel j'ai acheté un chapeau . . .*
>> the friend **for whom** I bought a hat . . .

> *la jeune fille pour laquelle j'ai fait une robe . . .*
>> the girl **for whom** I made a dress . . .

Lequel is used with a preposition if the pronoun refers to people or things. The form of *lequel* agrees in gender and number with the person(s) or thing(s) it refers to.

Note that if a preposition is involved and the pronoun refers to a thing, use only *lequel* (in its correct form).

> *l'argent avec lequel j'ai payé la facture . . .*
>> the money **with which** I paid the bill . . .

Quoi—Which or What

Quoi is used to refer to things only. It is usually used with a preposition when asking a question.

> *À quoi pensez-vous?*
>> **What** are you thinking of?

> *De quoi parlez-vous?*
>> **What** are you talking about?

De quoi is also used in many idiomatic expressions, such as:

[Sidebar left margin:]

If there is a preposition before the blank, you use *qui* if referring to a person, and the correct form of *lequel* if referring to a thing or a person. You never use *que* immediately following a preposition.

Lequel, laquelle, lesquels, and *l'esquelles,* are always used after the prepositions *entre, sans, parmi,* and *avant.*

avoir de quoi faire
> to have a lot to do

avoir de quoi manger
> to have something to eat

avoir de quoi vivre
> to have enough to live on

Merci beaucoup! Il n'y a pas de quoi!
> Many thanks! Don't mention it!

Ce à quoi—What

Ce à quoi is used to emphasize an idea, but it is mostly avoided otherwise.

Ce à quoi il faut toujours faire attention, c'est l'utilisation des pronoms.
> **What** you must always pay attention to is the use of pronouns.

Avec quoi—With What

Je voudrais savoir avec quoi il a fait cela.
> I would like to know **with what** he did this.

Sans quoi—Otherwise, If Not

Si tu fais tes devoirs tu pourras sortir; sans quoi tu resteras ici.
> If you do your homework, you can go out; **otherwise**, you'll stay here.

Dont—Of Whom or Of Which

Dont is correct only if the verb in the phrase is one that takes *de* as a preposition. *Dont* is always placed directly after the noun it replaces.

Le livre dont j'ai besoin est dans ma chambre.
> The book **that** I need is in my room.

L'ami dont elle a parlé viendra chez nous ce soir.
> The friend **of whom** she spoke will come to our house this evening.

When it is separated by a preposition, use *duquel, de laquelle, desquels, desquelles*.

L'homme à côté duquel le chien attend nous a salués.
> The man next to **whom** the dog waits greeted us.

Les gens à côté desquels nous étions assis n'ont pas arrêté de parler.
> The people next to **whom** we were sitting did not stop talking.

Ce dont—What

Ce dont is used as an object with a verb that takes the preposition *de*.

> *Il ne comprend pas ce dont j'ai besoin.*
>> He does not understand **what** I need.

> *J'ai oublié ce dont elle m'a parlé.*
>> I forgot **what** she talked to me about.

Now let's go back to our example first given on page 74.

Je n'ai pas le temps de faire les courses -------
ma mère m'a demandé de faire.

(A) qui
(B) que
(C) dont
(D) lesquelles

Here's How to Crack It

Is a preposition involved? No. Get rid of (D) *lesquelles*. You can also get rid of (A) *qui*, because where objects are concerned, *qui* is used only with a preposition.

Does *faire* take *de* as a preposition? No. Eliminate (C) *dont*. The answer must be (B) *que*.

Voilà l'ami ------- j'ai passé l'été.

(A) chez qui
(B) à qui
(C) que
(D) dont

Here's How to Crack It

Can *de* be used as a preposition following *passer l'été*? No. Eliminate (D).

Can *passer l'été* be used without a preposition? No. Eliminate (C) *que*.

Can *passer l'été* be used with *chez*? Yes. *Passer l'été chez* means "to spend the summer at the home of." (A) is the right answer.

You can use *à* with *passer l'été*, but in that case it would be used with a place, not with a person. Eliminate (B).

Où—Where

Voilà la bibliothèque où j'ai passé beaucoup de temps.
    There is the library **where** I spent a lot of time.

J'ai vu l'hôpital où je suis né.
    I saw the hospital **where** I was born.

Où can in many cases be replaced by *dans lequel* (*laquelle/lesquels/lesquelles*).

Où means **when** after the expressions *au moment, à l'époque, au temps,* and *le jour.* Use this carefully and only when it could be replaced by *pendant lequel.*

Les jours où il n'y avait plus de pain, ils mangeaient du riz.
    On the days **when** there was no more bread, they ate rice.

En—Of It/Of Them

En replaces a noun that is used with a verb that takes the preposition *de*. It can be used for people or things. It is often used in sentences that refer to a number or quantity of things.

Nous parlons du livre.
    We are speaking about the book.

Nous en parlons.
    We are speaking **about** it.

Où and *dans lequel* sometimes mean the same thing. You'll never be asked to choose between the two.

Think of *en* as meaning "of it" or "of them." You can use it in some cases where the *de* is understood but not actually used.

> *J'ai des cassettes.*
>> I have some tapes.
>
> *J'ai cinq cassettes.*
>> I have five tapes.
>
> *J'en ai cinq.*
>> I have five **of them**.

While *en* will usually refer to some kind of possession, it can also be used to indicate place or location if the verb in question uses *de*.

> *Il vient de Rome.*
>> He comes from Rome.
>
> *Il en vient.*
>> He's coming **from there**.

Y—There

Y often refers to place or location. *Y* replaces phrases that begin with prepositions that indicate place (*à, chez, dans, sur*).

> *Est-ce que tu vas à la fête?*
>> Are you going to the party?
>
> *Oui, j'y vais.*
>> Yes, I am going **there**.

Y, an indirect object pronoun, also replaces a thing or an idea that is preceded by the preposition *à*.

> *Tu crois au Père Noël?*
>> You believe in Santa?
>
> *Oui, j'y crois!*
>> Yes, I do!
>
> *Jouez-vous au tennis?*
>> Do you play tennis?
>
> *Oui, j'y joue.*
>> Yes, I do.
>
> *As-tu réfléchi à ta dissertation?*
>> Have you thought about your essay?

Oui, j'y ai réfléchi.
Yes, I have.

Chacun—Each One

Chacun à son tour!
Wait your turn!

On a trois euros chacun.
We each have three euros.

Quelques-uns/unes (de)—Some (Of)

Quelques-uns de ces livres sont à lire avant la fin du semestre.
Some of those books are to be read before the end of the semester.

Je peux goûter ces bonbons?
May I taste these candies?

Oui, prends en quelques-uns.
Yes, take **some of** them.

Aucun / Aucune—Not One, None

Je n'en aime aucun!
I like **none** of them!

Aucun and *aucune* are always used with *ne*.

Aucune de ces réponses n'est correcte.
None of these answers is correct.

Quelqu'un—Someone

Quelqu'un a volé ma moto!
Someone stole my motorcycle!

Personne—No One

Est-ce que quelqu'un a vu le voleur?
Did anyone see the thief?

Non, personne ne l'a vu.
No, **no one** saw him.

Like *aucun*, *personne* is used with *ne*. *Personne* can be used without the *ne* only if it is a one-word answer to a question.

Both *aucun* and *personne* must be used with *ne* in a sentence.

Qui a cassé ce vase?
Who broke this vase?

Personne.
No one.

Quelque chose—Something

*Je vous ai acheté **quelque chose** à la pâtisserie.*
I bought you **something** at the pastry shop.

Ne…rien—Nothing

Est-ce que tu as acheté quelque chose à la pâtisserie?
Did you buy something at the pastry shop?

*Non, je **n'ai rien** acheté.*
No, I did **not** buy **anything**.

———————————○———————————

Avez-vous des stylos? -------.

(A) Oui, lesquels.
(B) Oui, j'ai quelques.
(C) Non, je n'en ai aucun.
(D) Non, je n'ai pas.

Here's How to Crack It
(A) *lesquels* cannot stand by itself in a sentence unless it is an answer to a question (*Apporte-moi les stylos. Lesquels?*). Eliminate it.

(B) *quelques*, meaning "some," is an adjective and can only be used to modify a noun (*j'ai quelques stylos* or *j'en ai quelques-uns*). Eliminate it.

(C) *aucun* is used with *ne*. This is correct.

(D) By itself, *je n'ai pas* does not work. It lacks a reference to what it is that I do not have. To be correct, you would need to say either *je n'en ai pas* or *je n'ai pas de stylos*.

———————————○———————————

Qui va chercher le paquet à la poste? ------- vais.

(A) A Quoi
(B) J'y
(C) Personne
(D) J'en

Here's How to Crack It

Option (A), *A Quoi* does not work and makes no sense. It refers to things and is usually used with a preposition.

(B) is correct. The *y* replaces the expression *à la poste*.

(C) has two problems. First, *personne* needs to be used with *ne*. Second, *personne* takes the third person singular form of the verb (in this case, *va*).

(D) *En* is used to show either possession or to replace a noun that works with a verb that takes *de*. Here the verb is *aller* and it takes the preposition *à*. So *en* is not correct.

Since you're an expert by now, let's try tackling a full paragraph:

———————————○———————————

Hier, j'etais en train de ----(1)---- la maison quand j'ai vu à travers
la fenêtre un lapin sure la pelouse. Son corps ----(2)---- brun, mais
il avait des grades oreilles blanches. Je l'----(3)---- regardé pendant
quelques instants, puis en entendant un bruit il a ----(4)---- et en un
clien d'œil il a disparu.

1. (A) rouler
   (B) ranger
   (C) nager
   (D) hausser

2. (A) est
   (B) a été
   (C) serais
   (D) etait

3. (A) aie
   (B) ai
   (C) aura
   (D) airais

4. (A) choisi
   (B) établi
   (C) bondi
   (D) dormi

Here's How to Crack It

1. Which verb describes something that can be done in a house (*maison*)? *Rouler* means to roll, *ranger* means to tidy up, *nager* means to swim, and *hausser* means to raise. Only (B) makes sense in this context.

2. Which form of the verb *être* is correct here? Since the entire paragraph takes place in the past, we can eliminate both the present tense (A), *est*, and the conditional in (C), *serais*. Now we have to choose between the *passé composé* in (B) or the imperfect in (D). Because the sentence is describing specific characteristics of the rabbit (*lapin*), we need to use the imperfect, which is used to describe states of being that are ongoing. The fact that the other verb in the sentence is also imperfect (*avait*) is another hint that (D), *était*, is the right answer.

3. Which form of the verb *avoir* is correct here? Again, all action is taking place in the past, and the other verbs in the sentence both appear to use the *passé composé*. Eliminate the future, (C), and the conditional, (D). In (A) we have the subjunctive form, but since there isn't any uncertainty or emotion here, it's incorrect, which leaves (B) as the correct answer.

4. Which past participle has the correct meaning for the sentence? Translating the second half of the sentence, we learn that upon hearing a noise (*en entendant un bruit*), it (the rabbit) does something and in the blink of an eye, it disappears (*en un clien d'œil il a disparu*). (A) means the rabbit chose something, which doesn't fit. (B) doesn't work either, as the rabbit didn't establish anything. (C) is the past participle of *bondir*, which means to leap; this would be a logical thing for the rabbit to do. (D) suggests the rabbit slept, which isn't correct. (C) is the right answer.

Drill 1: Pronoun Questions

Answers can be found in Chapter 8.

1. ------- est arrivé à Paul hier?

   (A) Quel
   (B) Quoi
   (C) Qu'
   (D) Qu'est-ce qui

   no subj.

2. C'est -------.

   (A) eux
   (B) il
   (C) lui
   (D) le

3. C'est grâce à ------- que nous avons pu venir.

   (A) eux
   (B) les
   (C) leur
   (D) ils

4. La chose la plus difficile est de ------- réveiller le matin.

   (A) lui
   (B) il
   (C) le
   (D) moi

5. ------- a sorti la poubelle.

   (A) Il n'
   (B) Personne n'
   (C) Aucun
   (D) Qui

VERBS

There are three areas that verb questions tend to test: use of the subjunctive, agreement of the past participle, and tense.

Know the Subjunctive

About 25 percent of the grammar questions on the test deal with verb use. Over half of them ask you to decide whether or not to use the subjunctive.

What Is the Subjunctive?

Like the indicative, the subjunctive is not a tense; it is a mode or mood. While it is not often used in English, it is used very frequently in French. This is why it is always found on the SAT French Subject Test.

When Do You Use the Subjunctive?

In French and on the SAT French, you will use the subjunctive in phrases that follow expressions of doubt, suggestion, preference, desire, improbability, or emotion. The subjunctive is also used with certain conjunctions. All phrases that require use of the subjunctive will contain the word *que*.

Expressions That Take the Subjunctive

Doubt or Uncertainty

Je doute qu'il réussisse son examen.
> I **doubt that** he will pass his exam.

J'ai peur qu'il rate son examen.
> I **am afraid that** he will fail his exam.

Je ne crois pas que vous ayez raison.
> I **don't believe that** you are right.

Il est douteux qu'elle vienne ce weekend.
> It's **doubtful that** she will come this weekend.

Il est possible que j'aie tort.
> I may be wrong. (**It is possible that** I am wrong.)

You must use the indicative mode with verbs expressing an opinion, such as *penser que, croire que, espérer que, être sûr que, être certain que* when they are used in the affirmative form.

Je crois que vous avez raison.
> I believe you are right.

Nous pensons que tes parents seront contents de te revoir.
> We think your parents will be happy to see you again.

J'espère que vous allez bien.
> I hope you are well.

Compare the above examples to the following examples, which display these verbs used in the negative form. The negative form makes a difference!

Je ne crois pas qu'il ait raison.
> I don't think he's right.

Nous ne pensons pas que tes parents soient contents.
> We don't think your parents are happy.

Suggestion or Preference

All phrases that require use of the subjunctive will contain the word *que*.

Je préfère que vous rentriez tout de suite.
I **prefer that** you return at once.

Je tiens à ce que tu sois à l'heure.
I **insist that** you be on time.

Il vaut mieux que vous ne sortiez pas ce soir.
It is **better that** you do not go out tonight.

Il est important que vous étudiez l'emploi du subjonctif.
It is **important that** you study the use of the subjunctive.

Il faut que je prenne un rendez-vous chez le dentiste.
It is **necessary that** I make an appointment at the dentist's.

Desire

Je veux que tu travailles plus sérieusement.
I **want** you to work more seriously.

Je souhaite que tout se passe bien.
I **wish that** everything goes well.

Je désire qu'il soit heureux.
I **want** him to be happy.

Improbability

Il est peu probable qu'il neige demain.
It is **unlikely that** it will snow tomorrow.

Note: **Do not use the subjunctive with probability.**

Il est probable qu'il pleuvra demain.
It is **likely that** it will rain tomorrow.

Emotion

The subjunctive is used with expressions of doubt, preference, or emotion.

Je suis étonné qu'il ne soit pas encore là.
I **am surprised** that he is not yet here.

Je suis content que tout se soit bien passé.
I **am happy that** everything went well.

Je regrette que le temps passe si vite.
I **am sorry that** time goes by so quickly.

Superlative

Cet homme est le seul qui sache encore travailler de ses mains.
This man is the only one who still knows how to work with his hands.

C'est la meilleure nouvelle que vous puissiez lui donner.
It is the best news that you can give him.

Expressions That DO NOT Take the Subjunctive

The following expressions do not take the subjunctive when they are used in the **affirmative form only:**

il est probable que	it is likely
espérer	to hope
se demander	to wonder
croire	to believe
penser	to think
se douter que	to suspect

Il est probable qu'il neigera demain.
It is probably going to snow tomorrow.

Je me demande s'il viendra.
I wonder if he will come.

Beware of *ne* used as an expletive after *avant que, de peur que, de crainte que, avoir peur que, craindre que, à moins que.* **It is not a negative form.**

Je vais aller me promener avant qu'il ne pleuve.
I will go for a walk before it rains.

Je crains qu'il ne pleuve.
I am afraid it might rain.

Conjunctions That Take the Subjunctive

pour que, de manière (à ce) que	so that
de sorte que, afin que	so that
quoique, bien que	although
pourvu que, à condition que	provided that, so long as
à moins que	unless
jusqu'à ce que	until
en attendant que	waiting for
avant que (but not *après que*)	before
de crainte que, de peur que	for fear that
sans que	without
malgré que	even though, in spite of
pour autant que	as far as

Pay Attention to Improbabilities
Il est peu probable qu'il fasse beau demain.
It is unlikely to be beautiful tomorrow.

Conjunctions That DO NOT Take the Subjunctive

après que	after
dès que, aussitôt que	as soon as
pendant que	during
parce que	because
puisque	since
étant donné que	given that / with the understanding that
tandis que	while / whereas

So Now What?

You won't have to construct the subjunctive of a given verb; you only need to recognize it among the four answer choices. In addition to the present subjunctive, you may also see the past of the subjunctive. You'll recognize it because the auxiliary or helper verb (*avoir* or *être*) will be in the subjunctive. Note that with avoir, *il a* becomes *il ait* and with *être*, *il est* becomes *il soit*.

Present Tense

Certain:	*Je sais qu'il vient ce soir.*
	I know that he is coming tonight.
Uncertain:	*Je doute qu'il vienne ce soir.*
(Pres. Subj.)	I doubt that he is coming tonight.

Past Tense

Certain:	*Je sais qu'il est venu hier.*
	I know that he came yesterday.
Uncertain:	*Je doute qu'il soit venu hier.*
(Past Subj.)	I doubt that he came yesterday.

Now you try it:

Jean-Paul ne m'a pas téléphoné; j'ai peur qu'il
------- oublié notre rendez-vous.

(A) a
(B) avait
(C) ait
(D) aura

Here's How to Crack It

Does the expression *J'ai peur que* . . . take the subjunctive? Yes! It shows doubt, fear, or uncertainty. The answer is (C).

———————○———————

Try another one:

———————○———————

Ma mère m'a grondée quand elle ------- ma robe déchirée.

(A) voit
(B) a vu
(C) voie
(D) ait vu

Here's How to Crack It

Does the expression *Ma mère m'a grondée quand* . . . take the subjunctive?

No. The verb in this case (*voir*) is an actual event. Eliminate (C) and (D). This sentence requires the past, so the answer is (B). Also, note that we have *quand* here and not *que*.

———————○———————

———————○———————

Détruisez les preuves avant qu'il n'------- ce que nous avons fait.

(A) apprendra
(B) apprenne
(C) apprendrait
(D) apprend

Here's How to Crack It

Is *avant que* a conjunction that takes the subjunctive?

Yes. The answer is (B). (A) is the future. (C) is the conditional. (D) is the present.

———————○———————

Tense

You remember all those fancy verb tenses you learned in French class: the *passé simple*, the future perfect, the pluperfect subjunctive? Well, for the purposes of this test, you can forget them.

For the SAT French, you need to recognize the present, the imperfect, the *passé composé*, the future, the conditional, the past of the conditional, and the *plus-que-parfait*, and you must know when to use them. The subjunctive, actually a mode or mood rather than a tense, is the verb form most frequently tested. The conditional, also a mode or mood, is the next most frequently tested verb form.

Le Présent

This is pretty straightforward. It's the form of the verb you're most used to seeing.

> *Il part.*

L'Imparfait

The imperfect tense is a form of the past that indicates something was ongoing: either something that went on for a period of time in the past or something that happened repeatedly in the past.

présent	*imparfait*
Il part.	*Il partait.*

Le Passé Composé

This tense indicates that a past action (or state) is now complete. It is made up of an auxiliary verb (either *avoir* or *être* in the present tense) and a past participle. It indicates something that started and ended in the past and is now over.

présent	*passé composé*
Il part.	*Il est parti.*

Le Plus-Que-Parfait (Past Imperfect)

The past imperfect indicates that something happened in the past prior to another action in the past. It is made up of an auxiliary verb (*avoir* or *être* in the imperfect tense) and a past participle.

présent	*plus-que-parfait*
Il part.	*Il était parti.*

The *Passé Composé* vs. the *Imparfait*
Notice the difference between the *passé composé* and the imperfect. The *passé composé* describes a one-time action that is now complete, while the imperfect describes an action that was ongoing in the past.

Le Futur

This indicates that something will happen in the future.

présent   *futur*
  Il part.   *Il partira.*

Le Conditionnel

The conditional mode or mood is used to describe what people would do or what would happen if a set of conditions were met. In most cases it is used with another clause starting with *si*.

présent   *conditionnel*
  Il part.   *Si cela arrivait, il partirait.*
                                     Il partirait si cela arrivait.

The conditional is also used as a polite way of requesting things.

Je voudrais une baguette, s'il vous plaît, madame.
  I would like a baguette please, madame.

Use of the Conditional

Almost half of the questions that relate to verb sequence test you on the use of the conditional. The conditional is used in a sentence if there is a clause that begins with *si* and uses the imperfect tense.

si + imparfait → conditionnel

Si j'avais le temps, je le ferais moi-même.
  If I had the time, I would do it myself.

If the past imperfect is used, then the past conditional will be used.

si + plus-que-parfait → conditionnel passé

Si j'avais eu le temps, je l'aurais fait moi-même.
  If I had had the time, I would have done it myself.

Présent	Aujourd'hui, il fait ses devoirs.
Imparfait	Quand il était petit, il faisait ses devoirs.
Passé composé	Hier il a fait ses devoirs.
Plus-Que-Parfait	J'avais déjà fini mes devoirs quand il est parti.
Futur	Demain, il fera ses devoirs.
Conditionnel	S'il avait des devoirs, il les ferait.

The conditional is actually a mode or mood, not a tense. It is used to describe if/then situations.

You will use the conditional before or after clauses that start with *si* and contain the imperfect.

Sequence of Tenses

In questions with several verbs, the tenses and mode must follow a logical sequence.

- Sentences with a *si* clause:

Si clause	Result
`Imparfait	*conditionnel présent*
Si j'avais de l'argent	*j'achèterais un bateau.*
plus-que-parfait	*conditionnel passé*
Si j'avais eu de l'argent	*j'aurais fait ce voyage en Afrique.*

- Conjunctions referring to time such as *quand, une fois que, après que, lorsque, aussitôt que,* and *dès que* often require the use of the *futur antérieur* (future perfect) instead of the *futur simple.* You must consider whether:

1. In the sequence of future events, one action must be finished before the other can take place.

   Je pourrai répondre à ta question quand j'aurai parlé à mon frère.
   > I will be able to answer your question when I have talked to my brother.

2. In the future, the actions in both clauses will take place at the same time.

   Je vous appellerai quand il arrivera à la maison.
   > I will call you as soon as he arrives.

Je sortirai aussitôt que mon travail -------.

(A) finira
(B) serait fini
(C) sera fini
(D) finirait

Here's How to Crack It

What tense is correct? It is not a *si* clause or any form of politeness; therefore, it cannot be conditional mode. Eliminate (B) and (D). The conjunction *aussitôt que* indicates that one action has to take place before the other. Eliminate (A). (C) is the correct answer.

Si j'étais riche, je ------- un yacht.

(A) m'achète
(B) m'achèterai
(C) m'achetais
(D) m'achèterais

Here's How to Crack It

What tense is correct here? Because *si* is used with the imperfect, the following verb must be the conditional.

How do we recognize the conditional? It combines the structure of the future with the endings of the imperfect (*ais*, *ait*, etc.). (D) is the correct choice.

Avant d'entrer au restaurant, il m'a demandé si j'
------- assez d'argent pour payer le dîner.

(A) ai
(B) avais
(C) ai eu
(D) aurai

Here's How to Crack It

What tense is correct here? (A) cannot be correct. It is the present tense, and the previous clause, *il m'a demandé*, tells us the action is in the past. Since (D) is the future, we can eliminate it as well.

Do we use the imperfect or the past? (C) implies that having enough money was an event or action that occurred once prior to the question. Because we have the phrase, *avant d'entrer*, we know that the state of having money is an ongoing one, preceding and presumably continuing throughout dinner. (B) is the correct answer.

Make sure you can identify which tense (or mood) is which.

It is important that you recognize what each tense or mood looks like when you see it. Usually the ending of the verb will give you a clue.

Présent	Imparfait	Passé composé	Plus-que-parfait
je donne	je donnais	j'ai donné	j'avais donné
tu donnes	tu donnais	tu as donné	tu avais donné
il donne	il donnait	il a donné	il avait donné
nous donnons	nous donnions	nous avons donné	nous avions donné
vous donnez	vous donniez	vous avez donné	vous aviez donné
ils donnent	ils donnaient	ils ont donné	ils avaient donné

Futur	Conditionnel	Subjonctif présent	Conditionnel passé
je donnerai	je donnerais	que je donne	j'aurais donné
tu donneras	tu donnerais	que tu donnes	tu aurais donné
il donnera	il donnerait	qu'il donne	il aurait donné
nous donnerons	nous donnerions	que nous donnions	nous aurions donné
vous donnerez	vous donneriez	que vous donniez	vous auriez donné
ils donneront	ils donneraient	qu'ils donnent	ils auraient donné

With *donner*, as in all regular "*er*" verbs, the singular forms of the subjunctive present are identical to the indicative present.

AVOIR AND ÊTRE IN COMPOUND PAST TENSES

What Is an Auxiliary Verb?

It is a verb that loses its own meaning to help form a compound past tense for other verbs such as the *passé composé*, *plus-que-parfait*, *passé du subjonctif*, *conditionnel passé*, and *future antérieur*. Some verbs take either *avoir* or *être*. To make a sweeping generalization, **most verbs take *avoir***, but verbs that indicate a **change of place** (*aller, venir, partir*) **or state** (*naître, mourir, devenir…*) **and all reflexive verbs** (*se laver, se lever…*) take *être*. Sound tricky? Just remember Dr. and Mrs. Vandertramp.

Devenir	to become	Venir	to come
Revenir	to come back (with)	Aller	to go
&		Naître	to be born
Monter	to climb	Descendre	to go down
Rester	to stay	Entrer	to enter
Sortir	to go out	Rentrer	to come back
		Tomber	to fall
		Retourner	to return
		Arrive	to arrive
		Mourir	to die
		Partir	to leave

What Is a Past Participle?

A past participle is the form of the verb that combines with "to have" (in English), or *être* or *avoir* (in French), in order to make the past tense.

Je mange mon petit déjeuner.   *J'ai **mangé** mon petit déjeuner.*
    I eat my breakfast. (present)   I have eaten my breakfast. (past)

You'll most likely be given the choice of four different forms of the past participle—masculine singular, feminine singular, masculine plural, and feminine plural—with an occasional infinitive thrown in to confuse you. You must decide which is correct.

When Does the Past Participle Agree, and with What?

The past participle **agrees with the subject** of the sentence when:

- The verb takes *être* as its auxiliary verb and there is **no direct object placed after the verb.**

    Pauline et Chantal sont parties hier pour l'Afrique.
        Pauline and Chantal left for Africa yesterday.

- The verb is **reflexive** and therefore takes *être*, and there is **no direct object.**

    Elle s'est évanouie quand elle a entendu la nouvelle.
        She fainted when she heard the news.

The past participle **agrees with the direct object** of the sentence when:

- The **reflexive** verb has a **direct object placed before the verb.**

    La jambe qu'elle s'est cassée en skiant lui fait toujours mal.
        The leg she broke skiing is still painful.

- The verb takes *avoir* and has a **direct object placed before the verb.**

    La fille que nous avons vue au café est ma meilleure amie.
        The girl we saw in the café is my best friend.

The past participle will agree with the *subject* if the verb takes ***être*** or is reflexive.
It will agree with the *object* of the sentence if the verb takes ***avoir*** and the direct object is before the verb.

When Is There No Agreement?

- The **reflexive** verb has a **direct object** (usually a body part) **placed after the verb.**

Elle s'est piqué le doigt en cousant.
    She pricked her finger while sewing.

Elle s'est lavé les cheveux ce matin.
    She washed her hair this morning.

- The verb takes *avoir* and has a **direct object placed after the verb.**

J'ai vu ma meilleure amie au café aujourd'hui.
    I saw my best girlfriend in the café today.

Since questions in Part C often contain several sentences, information about the gender and number may come earlier than the sentence in which the blank appears.

Try this:

---○---

Les deux soeurs ⟨ont⟩ très bien ------- à l'université.

(A) réussi
(B) réussie
(C) réussis
(D) réussies

Here's How to Crack It

The verb *réussir* (to succeed, to be successful) uses the auxiliary verb *avoir.* Is there a direct object that precedes the verb? No. There is no direct object in this sentence. The correct answer is (A).

---○---

La fille à côté de moi m'a donné les renseignements dont j'avais besoin. Je l'ai ------.

(A) remercié
(B) remerciée
(C) remerciées
(D) remercier

la fille

Here's How to Crack It

The verb *remercier* (to thank) also takes *avoir* as its helper verb. Is there a direct object before the verb? Yes, "*l'*" refers to *la fille*. The correct answer is (B).

Oddball Verb Forms: Other Participles

There is a small chance that you will have a question or two on other participles: the present participle, the gerund, or the perfect participle. You don't need to know these terms—just be able to recognize how they work in a sentence. This type of question is most likely to appear on Part C, where you choose the appropriate form of the verb based on the sequence of tenses in the paragraph.

The Present Participle

The present participle is a verb form that ends in "-ing" in English. It shows that one action is happening at the same time as another.

> *J'ai vu les enfants courant sur la pelouse.*
> I saw the children running on the lawn.

The present participle "running" is also acting as an adjective, describing something about the children.

The Gerund

The gerund is also like an "-ing" verb form in English, but in this case, it is acting as an adverb rather than an adjective. In French, it is always accompanied by the preposition *en*. It can show:

- **That one action is happening at the same time as another**

> *Elle montait l'escalier en chantant.*
> She climbed the stairs while singing.

- **That one action is part of a process**

  En lisant, nous découvrons de nouveaux mondes.
    In reading, we discover new worlds.

- **That one action is part of a cause and effect**

  Eric apprend à danser en regardant des vidéos.
    Eric learns how to dance by watching videos.

The Perfect Participle

The perfect participle (made up of *ayant* or *étant* + the past participle) is the past tense of the present participle. An example in English would be "Having won the war, the army celebrated." This form is used to show that one action was completed before another began.

Ayant fini le repas, nous avons débarrassé la table.
    Having finished the meal, we cleared the table.

If the verb takes *être*, you will see *étant* instead of *ayant*:

Étant montée, elle ne pouvait plus entendre la discussion.
    Having gone upstairs, she could no longer hear the discussion.

Drill 2: Verb Questions

Answers can be found in Chapter 8.

1. Si -------, je préparerais le dîner.

    (A) vous en avez envie
    (B) on me le demande
    (C) j'avais le temps
    (D) tu seras d'accord

2. Paul regrette que nous ------- pas réussi.

    (A) n'avons
    (B) n'avions
    (C) n'ayons
    (D) n'aurons

3. ------- une lettre quand on a sonné à la porte.

    (A) J'écris
    (B) J'écrirais
    (C) J'écrive
    (D) J'écrivais

4. Elle n'a jamais oublié ce que nous ------- au moment de son départ.

    (A) disons
    (B) ayons dit
    (C) avons dit
    (D) aurions dit

5. Est-ce que vous ------- contents si je n'avais pas accepté l'invitation?

    (A) êtes
    (B) soyez
    (C) étiez
    (D) auriez été

6. Nous doutons ------- leur rendre visite chez eux.

    (A) qu'il ait le temps de
    (B) qu'il voudrait
    (C) qu'il peut
    (D) qu'elle avait envie de

7. -------, elle est partie pour le long trajet chez elle.

    (A) Disait au revoir
    (B) Dire au revoir
    (C) Ayant dit au revoir
    (D) Avoir dit au revoir

8. Tu pourras regarder la télé une fois que tu --------- ton travail.

    (A) aurais fini
    (B) finissais
    (C) auras fini
    (D) finisses

PREPOSITIONS

Below is a list of the most important prepositions for you to know.

Common Prepositions	
à	= to
de	= from, of
sur	= on
sous	= under
pour	= for
avant (+ nom)	= before
avant de (+ verbe)	= before
après	= after
chez	= at, to (location)
en	= of, in, from, to
dans	= in, into
entre	= between
pendant	= during
vers	= toward
sans	= without
sauf	= except, unless
selon	= according to
durant	= during
malgré, en dépit de	= in spite of
afin de	= in order to

Just as in English, certain verbs or expressions in French require prepositions while others require none. Memorization is the key here.

These questions will ask you for the preposition required. Some verbs can take more than one preposition depending on the meaning. In some questions, you will have the option of no preposition, denoted by a dash in the answer choice (——).

Il a refusé ------- faire son lit.

(A) ---
(B) à
(C) de
(D) sur

Out of context, *refuser* could take the preposition *à* or *de*, or no preposition at all. Each has a different meaning.

refuser quelque chose—to refuse something

> *Il a refusé l'offre.*
> He refused the offer.

refuser quelque chose à quelqu'un—to deny something to someone

> *Le juge a refusé les droits de visite à la mère.*
> The judge denied visitation rights to the father.

refuser de faire quelque chose—to refuse to do something

> *L'enfant a refusé de manger ses carottes.*
> The child refused to eat her carrots.

Which is appropriate for this question? Because someone is refusing to do something in this sentence, the correct answer is *de*, choice (C).

Back to Pronouns

Keep in mind that the verb's appropriate preposition may determine your choice of pronoun. If a verb requires a preposition in a given circumstance, for example, then you know that it takes an indirect and not a direct object. Or, if a given verb requires *de*, the relative pronoun used with it will reflect that.

C'est la robe ------- j'ai envie.

(A) que
(B) qui
(C) dont
(D) à qui

Your knowledge of prepositions will affect your choice of pronouns. For example, *dont* will only be a correct choice if the verb takes *de* as a preposition.

Here's How to Crack It

The verb *avoir envie* takes the preposition *de*. (A) can be eliminated because *que* is never used with a preposition. (B) can also be eliminated because *qui* cannot be a subject here (*j'* is the subject). *Avoir envie* takes *de*, so (D), which is used with *à*, cannot be right. (C) *dont* is correct because *dont* in a sense means *de + que*.

—————————◯—————————

Your experience studying French will probably provide you with a good sense of which verb takes which preposition, if you take the time to think about it. To refresh your memory, here is a partial list of verbs. Some never take a preposition, others sometimes take a preposition, and still others always take a preposition.

Verbs That Don't Take a Preposition

Verbs that don't take prepositions will be used with either the infinitive (the "to" form of a verb) or a direct object. Some verbs can be used with both.

pouvoir + **infinitive**	*Je peux faire n'importe quoi.* I can do anything I want.
espérer + **infinitive**	*J'espère venir demain.* I hope to come tomorrow.
vouloir + **infinitive**	*Je veux chanter.* I want to sing.
vouloir + **object**	*Je veux cette chemise.* I want this shirt.
mettre + **object**	*Il a mis le vase sur la table.* He put the vase on the table.
faire + **object**	*Marie a fait la vaisselle.* Marie washed the dishes.
acheter + **object**	*Il a acheté trois pantalons.* He bought three pairs of pants.

Verbs That Sometimes Take Prepositions and Sometimes Don't

aller + infinitive

Je vais chercher ma soeur à l'école.
I am going to get my sister at school.

aller à

Je vais aux États-Unis.
I am going to the United States.

refuser + object

Je refuse l'offre.
I refuse the offer.

refuser de

Je refuse de faire mes devoirs.
I refuse to do my homework.

oublier + noun

J'ai oublié mon stylo.
I forgot my pen.

oublier de

J'ai oublié de dire au revoir.
I forgot to say good-bye.

accepter + object

J'accepte votre invitation.
I accept your invitation.

accepter de

J'accepte de nettoyer la cuisine.
I agree to clean the kitchen.

compter + object

Je compte ma monnaie.
I am counting my change.

compter sur

Nous comptons sur vous pour nous aider.
We count on you to help us.

Verbs That Always Take Prepositions

réfléchir à

Je réfléchis à mon avenir.
I am thinking of my future.

penser à

Je pense à ma mère.
I am thinking of my mother.

penser de

Que pensez-vous du nouveau président?
What do you think of (about) the new president?

A good resource to have on hand is a verb book. A good verb book will tell you how to conjugate a given verb and which prepositions are used with that verb.

participer à	*Je participe aux Jeux Olympiques.* I am in the Olympic games.
assister à	*Est-ce que vous allez assister au concert?* Are you going to attend the concert?
faire attention à	*Faites attention aux assiettes en porcelaine!* Be careful with the porcelain plates!
répondre à	*Les élèves répondent aux questions du professeur.* The students answer the teacher's questions.
obéir à	*Le soldat obéit aux ordres.* The soldier obeys the orders.
parler de	*De quoi parlez-vous? Du chat?* What are you talking about? About the cat?
avoir peur de	*J'ai peur des araignées.* I am afraid of spiders.
risquer de	*Il risque de tomber.* He may fall.
venir de	*Je viens du supermarché.* I come from the supermarket.
avoir envie de	*J'ai envie d'un café.* I feel like having a coffee.
avoir besoin de	*J'ai besoin d'un crayon pour écrire.* I need a pencil to write.

Set Expressions

Certain rules govern the use of some prepositions.

When Discussing Going to a Country:

Je passe mes vacances . . .

Use *en* for feminine, singular countries.

> *en France*
> *en Italie*

Use *au* (*à* + *le*) for masculine, singular countries.

> *au Canada*
> *au Brésil*

Use *aux* (*à* + *les*) for plural countries, whether feminine or masculine.

> *aux États-Unis*
> *aux Bermudes*

When Discussing Being in or Going to a Town or City:

Je reste . . .
Je vais . . .

Use *à*:

> *à Paris*
> *à New York*
> *à Londres*

When Discussing Coming from a Country or Town:

Il est venu . . .

Use *de* or *des* for feminine countries.

> *de Russie*
> *d'Allemagne*
> *des Bermudes*

Use *du* or *des* for masculine countries.

> *du Japon*
> *des États-Unis*

Use *de* for all towns.

> *de Paris*
> *de Lyon*

You always use the preposition *à* when referring to being in or going to a city.

When discussing being in or going to the mountains or many American states, use *dans* + the definite article:
- dans les Alpes
- dans les Rocheuses
- dans le Vermont
- dans le Mississippi

List of Some Countries with Their Genders

Feminine	Masculine	Plural
la Russie	le Canada	les États-Unis (masc.)
la France	le Japon	les Pays-Bas (masc.)
l'Italie	le Brésil	les Bermudes (fem.)
l'Autriche	le Maroc	les Bahamas (fem.)
l'Allemagne	le Pérou	les Philippines (fem.)
la Belgique	le Viêt-Nam	
la Grèce	le Luxembourg	
la Roumanie	le Mexique	
l'Espagne	le Chili	
l'Angleterre	Le Liban	
l'Algérie	Le Sénégal	

Use of *en* and *de* + Name of Materials

To describe the material an object is made of, use either *de* or **en** + the name of the material.

un sac en cuir	a leather purse
un pot de terre	an earthenware pot
un mur de pierre	a stone wall
un pantalon en velours côtelé	corduroy pants
un collier de diamants	a diamond necklace
un bracelet en argent	a silver bracelet
une maison en brique	a brick house
une chaise en bois	a wooden chair
un fil de fer	a wire

Adverbs

You will want to be able to recognize French adverbs and not get puzzled by their various forms.

In English, most adverbs are formed with an adjective + the suffix **–ly**.

In French, most adverbs are formed with the feminine form of the adjective and the suffix **–ment**.

active	→	activement
ponctuelle	→	ponctuellement
calme	→	calmement

When the adjectives end with –*i*, –*ai*, –*u*, and –*é*, the adverbs are formed with the masculine form of the adjective.

vrai	→	*vraiment*
assidu	→	*assidûment*
poli	→	*poliment*

When the adjectives end with –*ant* or –*ent*, the endings of the adverbs change to –*mment*.

prudent	→	*prudemment*
négligent	→	*négligemment*
savant	→	*savamment*

Also remember that some irregular adverbs are different from the adjectives:

bon	→	*bien*
rapide	→	*vite*
meilleur	→	*mieux*
mauvais	→	*mal*

Be aware of certain adverbs placed as attributive adjectives. They do not agree with the nouns, of course, but you might mistakenly think they need to be eliminated because of their position in the sentence. Take a look at a few examples:

Il y a encore des places debout dans la salle de spectacle.
Mettez les bagages dans les coffres arrière.
Les roues avant sont à changer.

Drill 3: Preposition Questions

Answers can be found in Chapter 8.

1. Marie ------- les résultats de ses examens.

   (A) pense
   (B) attend
   (C) compte
   (D) a envie

2. Je ------- de leur écrire.

   (A) suis obligé
   (B) espère
   (C) veux
   (D) réfléchis

3. Je n'ai jamais eu l'occasion ------- voir ce film.

   (A) ---
   (B) à
   (C) de
   (D) sur

4. ------- le concert, elles bavardaient sans cesse.

   (A) Pendant
   (B) Dans
   (C) Avec
   (D) En

5. Je la vois souvent à -------.

   (A) France
   (B) ville
   (C) la boulangerie
   (D) loin

6. Elle n'a pas réfléchi ------- de refuser l'offre.

   (A) ---
   (B) avant
   (C) après
   (D) à

ODDS AND ENDS

At most, these topics will come up once or twice on the test.

Adjective Versus Adverb

Adjectives modify nouns. Adverbs modify verbs, adjectives, and other adverbs. In French, adverbs often end in *-ment*.

Odds and ends are just that: small, picky questions that show up from time to time but don't appear on every test.

> Elle a replacé le vase -------.
>
> (A) doux
> (B) brusquement
> (C) difficile
> (D) ennuyeuse

(A), (C), and (D) are all adjectives. (B) is the right answer.

When modifying an adjective, use the adverbs *trop*, *plus*, *très*, *si*, or *moins*.

Mieux, like *pire*, cannot be used to modify an adjective.

> Ce cassoulet est ------- bon.
>
> (A) mieux
> (B) sans
> (C) si
> (D) pas

Bon is an adjective. The word in the blank must be an adverb. Only *si* is an adverb that can be used to modify an adjective. (C) is the right answer.

Active Versus Passive

If you use *être* with the past participle of a verb that normally takes *avoir*, you are forming the passive tense of the verb.

Active (present)	Passive (present)
Le facteur distribue le courrier.	*Le courrier est distribué par le facteur.*
The postman delivers the mail.	The mail is delivered by the postman.

Possessive Adjectives

Possessive adjectives (not pronouns) show that a given noun belongs to a given person. But, unlike in English, French possessive adjectives agree with the gender and number of what is owned, not who owns it. The form of the adjective also changes depending on whether the noun begins with a vowel (or a silent "h").

Son is the masculine singular and *sa* is the feminine singular. **However, if a feminine noun begins with a vowel or a silent "h," the possessive adjective that goes with it will be** *son*. *Sa* **does not shorten to** *s'*.

> Elle avait de la soupe dans ------- assiette.
>
> (A) son
> (B) sa
> (C) s'
> (D) ses

Is *assiette* masculine or feminine? Singular or plural?P

Assiette is feminine, but the word begins with a vowel; you can't say *sa assiette*, so eliminate (B). Possessive adjectives don't contract, so eliminate (C). *Assiette* is singular; cancel (D), which is plural. (A) is the right answer.

Even though *amie* is feminine, you <u>can't</u> say *sa amie* or *s'amie*. When you have a feminine noun that begins with a vowel, it will take the masculine version of the possessive adjective—in this case, *son amie*. The College Board loves to ask this kind of question.

	Only one object		More than one object
	masculin	*féminin*	*masculin et féminin*
One owner	*mon livre*	*ma cravate*	*mes soeurs*
	ton frère	*ta santé*	*tes vacances*
	son amie	*sa voiture*	*ses cheveux*
	masculin et féminin		*masculin et féminin*
More than one owner	*notre professeur*		*nos voeux*
	votre chemise		*vos souhaits*
	leur voiture		*leurs cahiers*

SPECIAL POINTS FOR PART C

1. Is It Vocabulary or Grammar?

How can you tell? **A vocabulary question** will have **four words with clearly different meanings. A grammar question** will usually have **one word in four different forms** (for example, the same verb in four different tenses or with four different prepositions). When you see practice examples, the difference will be obvious.

2. Think of the Paragraph as a Whole

The paragraph is telling a story, so all sentences are connected. The key to this section is realizing that the correct answer can be based on both the sentence with the blank and on the sentences that precede it. You may even need to read past the blank sometimes in order to get a better understanding of what's going on. **Don't think of each sentence as a separate question.**

3. Special Grammar Points

Some grammatical points are tested more frequently in Part C than in Part B. All the following points are thoroughly discussed earlier in this chapter.

Verb Sequence

The **action** described in the paragraph must unfold **in a logical sequence. Make sure all the verbs** that you choose as answers **match the tense of the story.** Pay special attention to the rules for use of the imperfect and the conditional.

Agreement of the Past Participle

As we discussed earlier in this chapter, a past participle will agree with the *subject* if the verb takes *être*. If the verb takes *avoir* and the direct object comes before the verb, it will agree with the *object* of the sentence. In some cases, whether the direct object is masculine or feminine is revealed in a previous sentence.

SUMMARY

Questions in Parts B and C of the SAT French Subject Test evaluate your ability to choose correct words or expressions based on your understanding of French grammar. Here are the main grammar points you should review before the test:

Pronouns

Check which pronoun should be used in the sentence. Is it subject, direct object, indirect object, stressed, demonstrative, interrogative, reflexive, relative, indefinite, or another type of pronoun?

There are two kinds of pronoun questions on the test: one asks you to choose among the five main kinds of pronouns (subject, direct object, reflexive, indirect object, and stressed), and the other asks you to choose among pronouns like *qui, que, dont,* and *lequel.*

- Check its gender and number if needed (masculine, feminine, plural).
- Check whether it is also replacing a preposition.
- Check where it is placed in the sentence relative to the verb.

Verbs

Can you figure out the tense or mode, the use of the auxiliary verb, the agreement with the past participle, the tense sequence, or the specific use of certain verbs?

- Check the subject of the sentence.
- Check the tense sequence by looking at the meaning of the main clause.
- Check whether the verb takes *être* or *avoir* in compound past tense.
- Look at prepositions and conjunctions to help you decide what verb form or mode you should use.

Prepositions

Can you specify which one to use with which verb? What is the meaning when the preposition is combined with certain verbs and other words? How could it be replaced by a pronoun in a sentence?

- Check whether the verb takes *de* or *à*.
- Check whether the general meaning of the sentence indicates a place, a time, a cause, or something else.
- Check if the preposition is included in a pronoun form or if it should be transformed (*dont, auquel, duquel,* etc.).

Adverbs

Can you see the difference between adjectives and adverbs?

- Check the word's position in the sentence.
- Check the ending of the word and memorize the irregular adverb forms so you don't get tricked.

Practice Section

Answers can be found in Chapter 8.

Part B

Directions: Each of the following sentences contains a blank. From the four choices given, select the one that can be inserted in the blank to form a grammatically correct sentence. Choice (A) may consist of dashes that indicate that no insertion is required to form a grammatically correct sentence.

1. Marie a ------- à m'offrir.

   (A) quelque chose
   (B) rien
   (C) plusieurs
   (D) quelque

2. Claude ------- de faire les courses.

   (A) a rejeté
   (B) a aimé
   (C) est obligé
   (D) a voulu

3. C'est grâce à son ------- qu'il a réussi.

   (A) talents
   (B) amie
   (C) gentillesse
   (D) oncles

4. Je ferai la vaisselle -------.

   (A) avant de partir
   (B) à tout à l'heure
   (C) hier
   (D) jamais

5. C'est ------- qui a gagné!

   (A) personne
   (B) je
   (C) leur
   (D) elle

6. Nos voisins ------- aller à la piscine.

   (A) préfèrent
   (B) rêvent
   (C) plaisent
   (D) insistent

7. Je ------- demande s'il est temps de partir.

   (A) elle
   (B) moi
   (C) se
   (D) vous

8. Les dames sont arrivées avec -------.

   (A) leur
   (B) il
   (C) eux
   (D) les

9. La voiture verte est -------.

   (A) les leurs
   (B) la vôtre → yours
   (C) à aucun
   (D) ma

10. L'année dernière j'ai voyagé en -------.

    (A) Russie
    (B) États-Unis
    (C) New York
    (D) Canada

11. La réussite de ce projet est -------.

    (A) certainement
    (B) peu
    (C) probable
    (D) malgré

12. ------- ce soit fini.

    (A) Nous savons que
    (B) Il regrette que
    (C) Elle a oublié que
    (D) C'est lui qui a décidé que

13. C'est le collègue ------- j'ai beaucoup parlé.

    (A) dont
    (B) de quoi
    (C) sauf qui
    (D) avant que

parler de

14. ------- est le metteur en scène de ce film?

    (A) Quelle
    (B) Qu'est-ce qui
    (C) Où
    (D) Quoi

15. ------- avez-vous envie?

    (A) Quel
    (B) Y
    (C) Dont
    (D) De quoi

16. Le gouvernement ------- de négocier un accord.

    (A) va
    (B) espère
    (C) essaie
    (D) peut

17. ------- qu'il sache les nouvelles d'hier.

    (A) Sans doute
    (B) Je sais
    (C) Je crains
    (D) C'est à cause de Michel

18. Jean a réussi à trouver du travail ------- la grève.

    (A) afin de
    (B) lorsque
    (C) en dépit de
    (D) à moins de

19. -------, nous partirions.

    (A) Si elle en avait envie
    (B) Si tu peux
    (C) S'ils voudront
    (D) Si vous l'aviez permis

imp → condit

20. C'est le gâteau le plus délicieux -------.

    (A) que vous avez jamais mangé
    (B) qu'elle a jamais acheté
    (C) que nous avons jamais fait
    (D) que tu puisses jamais imaginer

subjunctive

Part C

Directions: The paragraphs below contain blank spaces indicating omissions in the text. For some blanks it is necessary to choose the completion that is most appropriate to the meaning of the passage; for other blanks, to choose the one completion that forms a grammatically correct sentence. In some instances, choice (A) may consist of dashes that indicate that no insertion is required to form a grammatically correct sentence. In each case, indicate your answer by filling in the corresponding oval on the answer sheet. Be sure to read each paragraph completely before answering the questions related to it.

Si j'avais su, ----(21)--- aller avec Marie et Christine. Trop tard, j'ai essayé de ----(22)---- téléphoner chez ----(23)---- mais ----(24)---- n'était là. ----(25)----, j'ai tenté de les retrouver au café. Quand ----(26)---- suis arrivé, je les ai ----(27)---- entrer ----(28)---- cinéma.

21. (A) je pouvais
    (B) j'avais pu
    (C) je peux
    (D) j'aurais pu

22. (A) elles
    (B) leur
    (C) eux
    (D) la

23. (A) elles
    (B) tu
    (C) leur
    (D) ils

24. (A) personne
    (B) une personne
    (C) rien
    (D) nulle

25. (A) Finalement
    (B) Terminé
    (C) Maintenant
    (D) Afin de

26. (A) j'en
    (B) j'y
    (C) je le
    (D) je me

27. (A) vu
    (B) vue
    (C) vus
    (D) vues

28. (A) à la
    (B) au
    (C) par la
    (D) par le

Avant ----(29)---- partir en vacances, Jean et Camille ont ----(30)---- à l'aéroport ----(31)---- demander ----(32)---- l'avion partait ----(33)----.

29. (A) ---
    (B) à
    (C) de
    (D) que

30. (A) téléphoné
    (B) téléphonée
    (C) téléphonés
    (D) téléphonées

31. (A) ---
    (B) à
    (C) de
    (D) pour

32. (A) si
    (B) quand
    (C) quel
    (D) qui

33. (A) en temps
    (B) chaque heure
    (C) à l'heure
    (D) de temps en temps

Chapter 6
Reading
Comprehension

For Reading Comprehension, Part D of the SAT French Subject Test, you will have to read passages in French and answer critical questions.

You will have anywhere from 4 to 6 literary or journalistic passages, each about 20 to 30 lines. In addition, you may see 1 to 3 ticket/schedule/advertisement-type texts; these may or may not be accompanied by pictures.

There is no clear order of difficulty in this section, so you will have to use your judgment to determine which questions you are going to answer.

It is best to read the questions first so you have a better sense of what to look for as you read the passages. The passages are generally quite short. Read them through at a moderate pace to get the general idea of what the passage is about. Do not become obsessed if you don't understand every word or sentence, and keep an eye out for trap answers.

Get acquainted with the format of the test. Follow the suggestions we give you and then try the practice section at the end of this chapter.

PART D: READING COMPREHENSION

Pace Yourself

Do not be anxious about this section. There is no clear order of difficulty, so just go to the next question if you find something too difficult and then go back if you have time. The short passages are not necessarily easier than the long ones, so make sure you choose wisely.

The Questions Are in Order

Reading the questions first will give you an idea of what you are about to read and what to look for. Use the fact that the questions are in roughly chronological order to help you find the answers in the passage.

The questions on reading comprehension go in order of the text. The early questions relate to information early in the passage. Later questions refer to information that appears later in the passage.

Go Back

Once you have an idea of what the answer is, go back to the passage and make sure you are not falling for a trap answer. Reread the entire sentence or group of sentences that relate to the question to make sure you have evidence for your answer.

Use Process of Elimination: POE

Common Sense

You can eliminate answers that don't make sense in the context of the passage.

Familiar Words—Wrong Context

Sometimes the words in an answer choice will be strongly reminiscent of the words used in the passage. If a word or phrase is directly lifted from the passage, be careful—you may be falling into a trap.

Misleading Look-Alikes

Sometimes, instead of repeating words verbatim, the College Board will take a word and twist it subtly. For example, if the word *errer* appears, they might have a trap answer choice containing the word *erreur*.

What Is This Weird Tense?

In formal French, literary writing uses a tense called the *passé simple* (or past historic) instead of the *passé composé*. You don't need to know how to conjugate it or when to use it. You simply need to recognize which verb is being used.

Present	Past Participle	Passé Simple
il donne	*donné*	*il donna*
il croit	*cru*	*il crut*
il met	*mis*	*il mit*

You should be able to recognize the *passé simple* forms of some commonly used French verbs, such as *aller, avoir, dire, être, faire, lire, metter, pouvoir, prendre, savoir, venir, vouloir.*

Try the following passage, looking for the types of trap answers mentioned above.

Part D

Directions: Read the following selections carefully for comprehension. Each selection is followed by a number of questions or incomplete statements. Select the completion or answer that is best according to the text and fill in the corresponding oval on the answer sheet.

Ligne

La cité elle-même, on doit l'avouer, est laide. D'aspect tranquille, il faut quelque temps pour apercevoir ce qui la rend différente de tant d'autres villes commerçantes, sous toutes les
5   latitudes. Comment faire imaginer, par exemple, une ville sans pigeons, sans arbres et sans jardins, où l'on ne rencontre ni battements d'ailes ni froissements de feuilles, un lieu neutre pour tout dire? Le changement des saisons ne s'y lit que
10   dans le ciel. Le printemps s'annonce seulement par la qualité de l'air ou par les corbeilles de fleurs que des petits vendeurs ramènent des banlieues; c'est un printemps qu'on vend sur les marchés. Pendant l'été, le soleil incendie les mai-
15   sons trop sèches et couvre les murs d'une cendre grise; on ne peut plus vivre alors que dans l'ombre des volets clos. En automne, c'est, au contraire,

The best way to get the right answer is to take the time to go back and carefully reread the sentence or sentences that relate to the question.

un déluge de boue. Les beaux jours viennent
seulement en hiver.
(Camus, *La Peste*, Folio)

1. Ce passage nous décrit

   (A) une ville idéale
   (B) un marché en ville
   (C) le changement des saisons
   (D) les attributs principaux d'une cité

2. Qu'est-ce qui rend la cité différente des autres villes?

   (A) La présence des pigeons
   (B) La latitude
   (C) Le manque de verdure et d'oiseaux
   (D) La couleur du ciel

3. Aux lignes 13-14, "c'est un printemps qu'on vend sur les marchés" veut dire

   (A) qu'on peut tout acheter au marché
   (B) qu'on sait que le printemps est arrivé quand on peut acheter des fleurs
   (C) qu'on voit mieux le printemps dans les banlieues
   (D) que le printemps est comme un marché

4. Comment réagissent les habitants de la ville à l'arrivée de l'été?

   (A) Ils font des feux.
   (B) Ils se plaignent.
   (C) Ils restent à l'intérieur.
   (D) Ils deviennent des voleurs.

Don't be afraid to eliminate answer choices that don't make sense.

Here's How to Crack It

1. Ce passage nous décrit

   (A) une ville idéale
   (B) un marché en ville
   (C) le changement des saisons
   (D) les attributs principaux d'une cité

You are asked to choose what the passage describes:

(A) "an ideal town" is a misunderstanding of the first sentence. The first sentence tells us that the city is ugly, and the passage goes on to list primarily negative qualities. Eliminate this choice.

(B) "a marketplace in town" is an example of familiar words / wrong context. The word *marché* appears, as does the word *vendeurs*; however, the passage as a whole is not about the market. This choice is too specific. Eliminate it.

(C) "the changing of the seasons" is another example of familiar words—wrong context. The change of seasons is discussed, but again, it is too specific for this question.

(D) **"the principal attributes of a town" is the correct answer.** The passage discusses several distinctive features of a city.

> 2. Qu'est-ce qui rend la cité différente des autres villes?
>
>   (A) La présence des pigeons
>   (B) La latitude
>   (C) Le manque de verdure et d'oiseaux
>   (D) La couleur du ciel

You are asked to choose what makes the city different from other cities. The answer is in the section that starts with the second sentence of the passage.

(A) "the presence of pigeons" is an example of familiar words—wrong context. Pigeons are mentioned, but what is significant is their absence.

Watch out for answers that use familiar words from the passage out of context.

(B) "the latitude" is another example of familiar words—wrong context. The word "latitude" appears in the second sentence, but it is used to describe the location of other cities, in any latitude.

(C) **"the lack of greenery and birds" is the correct answer.** Notice that it paraphrases part of the third sentence: *sans pigeons, sans arbres et sans jardins.*

(D) "the color of the sky" takes the word *ciel* out of context. It is a misunderstanding of the sentence: *Le changement des saisons ne s'y lit que dans le ciel.*

> 3. Aux lignes 13-14, "c'est un printemps qu'on vend sur les marchés" veut dire
>
>   (A) qu'on peut tout acheter au marché
>   (B) qu'on sait que le printemps est arrivé quand on peut acheter des fleurs
>   (C) qu'on voit mieux le printemps dans les banlieues
>   (D) que le printemps est comme un marché

You are asked to interpret the sentence "it is a spring that is sold in the marketplace" within the context of the passage.

(A) "that one can buy everything at the market" is too literal and does not relate to the passage.

(B) **"that one knows spring has arrived when one can buy flowers" is the correct answer.** It corroborates the meaning, connecting it to the previous sentence about how few signs there are of the change of seasons.

(C) "that it is easier to see the spring in the suburbs" takes the word *banlieues* out of context.

(D) "that spring is like a marketplace" is a literal interpretation.

4. Comment réagissent les habitants de la ville à l'arrivée de l'été?

   (A) Ils font des feux.
   (B) Ils se plaignent.
   (C) Ils restent à l'intérieur.
   (D) Ils deviennent des voleurs.

"How do the inhabitants of the town react to the arrival of summer?" This topic is discussed in the next-to-last sentence of the passage.

(A) "They make fires" misinterprets the phrase "*le soleil incendie les maisons.*"

(B) "They complain" comes out of the blue. Complaining is not discussed anywhere in the passage.

(C) **"They stay indoors" is the correct answer.** This is what the sentence "*on ne peut plus vivre alors que dans l'ombre des volets clos,*" implies—"then one can only live in the shade of closed shutters."

(D) "They become thieves" is an example of a misleading look-alike. Here the word *volets* (shutters) has been twisted into the word *voleurs.*

TICKETS/SCHEDULES/ADVERTISEMENTS

These graphical passages can be a blessing because you have less to read and because common sense works so well. **Pay special attention to the small print.**

- Read through the schedule or advertisement.
- Get a sense of the layout. Read all sizes of print.
- Use your common sense.
- Eliminate misleading look-alike words.

les jeunes aiment l'argent

Ils aiment l'argent signé Ravinet d'Enfert
Ravinet d'Enfert a créé, en métal argenté, une collection contemporaine de qualité. Héritier d'une longue tradition, éditeur d'une collection classique très réputée, Ravinet d'Enfert propose des créations de notre temps comme les services "Président" et "Brantôme." Ravinet d'Enfert les présente avec des couverts, des plats, des luminaires et des accessoires de table dans son catalogue "lignes actuelles."
Demandez-le dans les magasins ou à l'aide du bon à découper qui se trouve à droite.

RAVINET D'ENFERT
83, RUE DU TEMPLE—PARIS—3e

Veuillez m'adresser gratuitement vos catalogues
○ tradition
○ lignes actuelles

Nom _____
Prénom _____
Adresse _____

The Small Print
On ticket/schedule/advertisement-type questions, pay special attention to the small print and the titles!

1. Selon la publicité, les services "Président" et "Brantôme"

   (A) sont d'une collection classique
   (B) coûtent beaucoup d'argent
   (C) sont très réputés
   (D) sont d'un style contemporain

2. Le bon à découper vous offre

   (A) des produits gratuits
   (B) un choix de catalogues
   (C) des adresses
   (D) une description de nouvelles lignes

Here's How to Crack It

1. Selon la publicité, les services "Président" et "Brantôme"

   (A) sont d'une collection classique
   (B) coûtent beaucoup d'argent
   (C) sont très réputés
   (D) sont d'un style contemporain

"According to the advertisement, the '*Président*' and '*Brantôme*' collections . . . "

(A) "are from a classic collection" takes a phrase out of context. The company produces a traditional line, but these styles, in contrast, are modern.

(B) "cost a lot of money" is also out of context. *Argent* is used here to mean "silver," not "money." This answer could be true, but there is no evidence of it in the ad.

(C) "have a good reputation" is also out of context. Again, the company is renowned, but we don't know about these specific lines.

(D) "are of a contemporary design" is the correct answer. Notice that it paraphrases the actual description *des créations de notre temps*.

2. Le bon à découper vous offre

   (A) des produits gratuits
   (B) un choix de catalogues
   (C) des adresses
   (D) une description de nouvelles lignes

"The coupon offers you . . . "

Le bon à découper vous offre refers to the coupon in the corner.

(A) "free products" is a familiar word, but it's in the wrong context. The catalog is free; the products are not.

(B) "a choice of catalogs" is the correct answer. The two boxes name two types of catalogs.

(C) "addresses" is a familiar word—wrong context. *Adresser* is part of a request to the company to send or address a catalog to the reader.

(D) "a description of new lines" is not terrible, but is not as good as choice (B). The coupon itself is not providing an actual description of the contemporary lines.

Practice Section

Answers can be found in Chapter 8.

Part D

Directions: Read the following selections carefully for comprehension. Each selection is followed by a number of questions or incomplete statements. Select the completion or answer that is best according to the text and fill in the corresponding oval on the answer sheet.

Chez Rasseneur, après avoir mangé une soupe, Etienne, remonté dans l'étroite chambre qu'il allait occuper sous le toit, en face du Voreux, était tombé sur son lit, tout vêtu, assommé de fatigue. En deux jours, il n'avait pas dormi quatre heures. Quand il s'éveilla, au crépuscule, il resta étourdi un instant, sans reconnaître le lieu où il se trouvait; et il éprouvait un tel malaise, une telle pesanteur de tête, qu'il se mit péniblement debout, avec l'idée de prendre l'air, avant de dîner et de se coucher pour la nuit.
(Zola, *Germinal*, Garnier)

Ligne

5

1. Etienne n'avait pas l'énergie de

   (A) dormir
   (B) se déshabiller
   (C) manger
   (D) mettre ses habits

2. Selon le passage, pour quelle raison Etienne est-il fatigué?

   (A) Il a trop mangé.
   (B) Il n'a pas dormi du tout depuis deux jours.
   (C) Il s'est couché à quatre heures du matin.
   (D) Il n'a dormi que quelques heures en 48 heures.

3. A quel moment de la journée s'est-il réveillé?

   (A) Tôt le matin
   (B) À midi
   (C) Tôt le soir
   (D) À minuit

4. Comment réagit-il au moment de se réveiller?

   (A) Il ne se souvient pas où il est.
   (B) Il ne trouve pas ses habits.
   (C) Il se sent en retard.
   (D) Il a faim.

5. Que voulait-il faire avant de dîner?

   (A) Respirer
   (B) Se promener
   (C) S'éveiller
   (D) Courir

Chaque dimanche, avant la guerre, Morissot partait dès l'aurore, une canne en bambou d'une main, une boîte en fer-blanc sur le dos. Il prenait le chemin de fer d'Argenteuil, descendait à Colombes, puis gagnait à pied l'île Marante. A peine arrivé en ce lieu de ses rêves, il se mettait à pêcher; il pêchait jusqu'à la nuit.

Chaque dimanche, il rencontrait là un petit homme replet et jovial, M. Sauvage, mercier, rue Notre-Dame-de-Lorette, un autre pêcheur fanatique. Ils passaient souvent une demi-journée à côté, la ligne à la main et les pieds ballants au-dessus du courant; et ils s'étaient pris d'amitié l'un pour l'autre.

(Guy de Maupassant, *Deux Amis*, Le Livre de Poche)

6. Quand Morissot partait-il pour l'île?

(A) Après le coucher du soleil
(B) Au moment du coucher du soleil
(C) Au moment du lever du soleil
(D) L'après-midi

7. Comment gagnait-il l'île?

(A) En autobus et à pied
(B) En bateau
(C) En voiture et à pied
(D) En train et à pied

8. A quel moment commençait-il à pêcher?

(A) Pratiquement au moment où il arrivait
(B) Au moment où il commençait à rêver
(C) À la tombée de la nuit
(D) Quand son ami arrivait

9. Qu'est-ce qui se trouvait dans la rue Notre-Dame-de-Lorette?

(A) L'île Marante
(B) L'endroit où les deux amis se rencontraient
(C) Le magasin de M. Sauvage
(D) La gare

Claire.—Tes parents t'interdisent-ils d'aller voir un film?

Guillaume.—Non, puisque je leur demande ce qu'ils en pensent. Quelquefois, ils me disent: "Il vaut mieux que tu ailles voir un autre film."

Claire.—Moi, mes parents pensent qu'à mon âge, le cinéma n'est pas très bon, de toute façon.

Gilles.—Tu n'y vas jamais, alors?

Claire.—Si, mais en cachette.

Guillaume.—Ça alors, moi je ne le ferai jamais . . . Je ne peux pas mentir à mes parents. Je crois que je me sens libre parce que mes parents pensent que c'est un peu à moi de choisir, mais pas n'importe quoi.

(*Pour ou contre*, Hachette)

10. Les parents de Guillaume

(A) lui conseillent de ne jamais aller au cinéma
(B) ne sont pas concernés par ce qu'il fait
(C) n'aiment pas le cinéma
(D) lui donnent leur avis sur les films qu'il choisit

11. A la question de Gilles, Claire répond

(A) qu'elle ne va jamais au cinéma
(B) qu'elle va au cinéma si ses parents sont d'accord
(C) qu'elle va au cinéma sans le dire à ses parents
(D) qu'elle va souvent au cinéma

12. Quelle raison Guillaume donne-t-il pour ne pas mentir à ses parents?

(A) Ses parents le laissent faire n'importe quoi.
(B) Ses parents lui donnent la responsabilité de décider que faire.
(C) Il vaut mieux ne pas le faire.
(D) Ses parents n'aiment pas le cinéma.

Attention! Dans le 5e, le boulevard Saint-Michel et la place Saint-André-des-Arts ne sont plus fréquentables! Les petits bars sympathiques et les restaurants à petits prix ont disparu au profit d'établissements prétentieux où un personnel pressé sert des bières à la chaîne. On débite des sandwiches sous cellophane, des frites et, signe des temps, McDonald et Wimpy se font face, à deux pas du Luxembourg. Cinémas et librairies semblent résister, pour l'instant, à cette invasion "made in U.S." Les jeunes se pressent chez "Gibert" et dans les salles d'art et d'essai où passent les vieux films d'hier et ceux d'avant-garde. Pour se rencontrer, les jeunes préfèrent les petites rues plus anonymes, les petits restaurants à six ou sept tables, les bars sans faux clinquant que l'on trouve autour du Panthéon.
(*Paris*, Hachette)

13. L'auteur réagit au changement sur le boulevard Saint-Michel et sur la place Saint-André-des-Arts avec

   (A) impatience
   (B) regret
   (C) indifférence
   (D) plaisir

14. Qu'est-ce qu'on trouve près du Luxembourg?

   (A) Des petits restaurants anonymes
   (B) Des cafés sympathiques
   (C) Des librairies prétentieuses
   (D) Des établissements américains

15. D'après le passage, on comprend que "Gibert" est

   (A) un film
   (B) un café
   (C) une librairie
   (D) un musée

16. Que font les jeunes au lieu d'aller boulevard Saint-Michel?

   (A) Ils fréquentent la place Saint-André-des-Arts.
   (B) Ils sont pressés d'aller voir des films américains.
   (C) Ils cherchent des bars sympathiques dans un autre endroit.
   (D) Ils résistent à l'envie d'aller dans les librairies.

Je n'ai rien à cacher. J'étais orpheline et pauvre, j'élevais mon frère cadet. Un vieil ami de mon père m'a demandé ma main. Il était riche et bon, j'ai accepté. Qu'auriez-vous fait à ma place? Mon frère était malade et sa santé réclamait les plus grands soins. J'ai vécu six ans avec mon mari sans un nuage. Il y a deux ans, j'ai rencontré celui que je devais aimer. Nous nous sommes reconnus tout de suite, il voulait que je parte avec lui et j'ai refusé.
(Sartre, *Huis-clos*, Folio)

17. La narratrice donne à entendre qu'elle

   (A) travaillait beaucoup
   (B) était invalide
   (C) avait beaucoup de soucis
   (D) s'était mariée avec l'ami de son père

18. Le frère de la narratrice

   (A) a vécu avec elle pendant six ans
   (B) était plus jeune qu'elle
   (C) était soldat
   (D) n'aimait pas son mari

19. Le passage nous donne l'impression

   (A) qu'elle voulait défendre ses actions
   (B) que son mari lui manquait
   (C) que son frère était guéri
   (D) qu'elle aimait le beau temps

20. Après six ans, qu'est-ce qui s'est passé?

   (A) Le mari de la narratrice est parti.
   (B) Le beau temps a changé.
   (C) La narratrice a décidé de partir.
   (D) La narratrice a trouvé un amant.

Antoine Lemurier, qui avait manqué mourir, sortit
heureusement de maladie, reprit son service au bureau,
Ligne et, tant bien que mal, pansa ses plaies d'argent. Durant
cette épreuve, les voisins s'étaient réjouis en pensant que
5 le mari allait crever, le mobilier être vendu, la femme à la
rue. Tous étaient d'ailleurs d'excellentes gens, des cœurs
d'or, comme tout le monde, et n'en voulaient nullement au
ménage Lemurier, mais voyant se jouer auprès d'eux une
sombre tragédie avec rebonds, péripéties, beuglements
10 de proprio, huissier et fièvre montante, ils vivaient
anxieusement dans l'attente d'un dénouement qui fût
digne de la pièce.
(Marcel Aymé, *Les Sabines*, Folio)

21. On comprend qu'Antoine Lemurier

    (A) est mort
    (B) a raté le train
    (C) a quitté son bureau
    (D) a failli succomber à une maladie

22. Qu'est-ce que les voisins pensaient de la maladie de
    Lemurier?

    (A) Ils attendaient une fin intéressante à la tragédie.
    (B) Ils étaient tristes.
    (C) Ils étaient fâchés contre Lemurier.
    (D) Ils tombaient malades.

23. Selon les voisins, qu'est-ce qui serait "un
    dénouement . . . digne" de la situation?

    (A) M. Lemurier perd son travail.
    (B) M. Lemurier récupère complètement.
    (C) Mme Lemurier est sans abri.
    (D) Mme Lemurier vend la maison.

Summary

For Part D, Reading Comprehension, practice is the best way to improve your score. Make sure you do the following:

- o Memorize the instructions to save time on test day.

- o Read the questions first so you know what to look for in the passage.

- o Read and eliminate wrong answer choices.

- o Do not get stuck on difficult passages or questions. Move on and come back later if you have the time.

Chapter 7
French Listening

The SAT French Subject Test with Listening evaluates your reading and listening skills of spoken French. It is about one hour long.

The test is currently administered in November at designated test centers. You will need to fill out a special registration form and find the testing center nearest to you. On test day, you must bring an appropriate CD player with earphones.

In this chapter, we explore the overall structure and describe each part of the listening test.

OVERALL STRUCTURE OF THE LISTENING TEST

The SAT French Subject Test with Listening consists of **40 minutes of reading (written questions)** and **20 minutes of listening (oral questions)**, with 85 to 90 questions in all. This means that about two-thirds of the SAT French Subject Test with Listening consists of questions we've already discussed. You will have 40 minutes to work on those. There are, however, fewer of each type.

- Part A—Vocabulary Completions: 12–16 questions
- Part B—Grammar Blanks: 12–16 questions
- Part C—Paragraph Blanks: 15–17 questions
- Part D—Reading Comprehension: 20–25 questions

In addition to those regular questions, you will have 20 minutes to work on the listening part of the test. There will be three parts with a total of about 40 questions covering pictures (8–12 questions), dialogues (10–12 questions), and monologues (10–15 questions):

- Listening—Part A: Pictures
- Listening—Part B: Short Dialogues and Monologues
- Listening—Part C: Longer Dialogues and Monologues

Samples of each type of question are available on the College Board's website, www.collegeboard.com.

Should You Sign Up for the French Subject Test with Listening?

The results of your test will give colleges a more complete picture of your French language proficiency. Your aim should be to give them the best picture of your abilities for the purpose of class placement.

You do not have to speak French on either of the SAT French Subject Tests. Therefore, do not feel anxious about the listening portion of the test. Many students tend to do better on this section than they do on the written portion. There are fewer grammar and reading questions, which will benefit students who are better at spoken French than at grammar or reading comprehension. To prepare for the listening test you may want to visit www.collegeboard.com, as mentioned above, and practice with www.laguinguette.com. You'll also find it helpful to watch and listen to French TV news and as many French movies as you can get your hands on.

LISTENING—PART A: PICTURES

The first part of the Listening Test consists of choosing which spoken phrase best matches the provided picture. Each sentence will be designated (A), (B), (C), or (D).

Directions: For each item in this part, you will hear four sentences designated (A), (B), (C), and (D). They will not be printed in your test booklet. As you listen, look at the picture in your test booklet and select the choice that best reflects what you see in the picture or what someone in the picture might say. Then fill in the corresponding oval on the answer sheet. You will hear the choices only once. Now look at the following example.

Look at the picture before the answer choices are played. Get a general idea of what is going on.

Make a Decision as You Hear Each Choice

As each answer choice is read to you, decide if that choice is at all appropriate. If it is not, cross out that choice on your answer sheet. You may not be allowed to write in your book. If the choice is good or possible, make a small mark inside the bubble. Probably only one will make any sense. If not, guess. **Don't wait to hear all the choices before deciding about each of them.** Decide "yes" or "no" as you go, for will only hear each choice one time, so you must think quickly. Erase all stray marks once you select an answer.

LISTENING—PART B: SHORT DIALOGUES

On this section you will hear either a dialogue between two people, or a monologue. It will be followed by three answer choices labeled (A), (B), or (C). The answer choices will be heard only once. Again, listen closely because nothing is repeated.

Directions: In this part of the test you will hear several short selections. A tone will announce each new selection. The selections will not be printed in your test booklet, and will be heard only once. At the end of each selection, you will be asked one or two questions about what was said, each followed by three possible answers, (A), (B), and (C). The answers are not printed in your test booklet. You will hear them only once. Select the **BEST** answer and fill in the corresponding oval on the answer sheet. Now listen to the following example, but do not mark the answer on your answer sheet.

Make a Decision as You Hear Each Choice

As you hear each answer choice, decide if it is appropriate or not. Eliminate it or keep it on your answer sheet. Once you've selected an answer, erase all stray marks. Do not mark (D) or (E) as choices.

LISTENING—PART C: LONG PASSAGES

Hear Ye, Hear Ye
On Part C of the listening part of the test, answer the questions as you hear the information being presented. Don't wait to hear the whole thing!

This section consists of longer monologues or dialogues that will be heard only once. In this section, the questions and the four answer choices will be in the test booklet.

Directions: You will now hear some extended dialogues or monologues. You will hear each only once. After each dialogue or monologue, you will be asked several questions about what you have just heard. These questions are also printed in your test booklet. Select the best answer to each question from among the four choices printed in your test booklet and fill in the corresponding oval on the answer sheet. There is no sample question for this part.

Forewarned, Forearmed

The great thing about this question type in Part C is that the questions and answer choices are printed in your booklet. As the instructions are being read (familiarize yourself with them now so that you don't waste time on the big day) and before the passage is read, read the questions and their answers to get a sense of the topic.

As in reading comprehension, the questions are in chronological order. Don't wait for the entire passage to be read before answering the questions. (It would be hard for even a native speaker to remember all those details for so long.) As the passage is being read, look at each question and mark the correct answer as soon as you hear it. The questions will either ask you to repeat specific details or paraphrase them. You are not required to interpret or infer.

Summary

Practice is the number one way to improve your score on the SAT French Listening Test. In order to get your best score, make sure you do the following:

o   Memorize the instructions to save time on test day.

o   Bring the required CD player and fresh batteries.

o   Come rested and well fed.

o   Follow the pace of the recording.

o   Make your decision as you hear the choices because you won't remember them if you wait.

o   If there is a picture, look at all the details.

o   On the Long Passages section, do not wait for the entire passage to be read. Answer as soon as you figure out the right choice.

Part III
Drill Answers and
Explanations

8   Drill Answers and Explanations

Chapter 8
Drill Answers and Explanations

CHAPTER 3

DRILL 1

une usine	a factory
la honte	the shame
l'œuvre	the work
en vouloir à	to be angry at, to have a grudge against
mou	soft, limp, listless
taquiner	to tease
la foule	the crowd
ramasser	to gather, to pick up
soutenir	to support, to sustain
repasser	to come back, to cross again, to iron
se méfier de	to mistrust, to be suspicious
se débarrasser de	to get rid of

DRILL 2

évaluer	to evaluate
sacré	sacred
retarder	to delay, to slow down
fréquenter	to go somewhere frequently, to see someone on a regular basis
nombre	number
assurer	to assure
raison	reason
plante	plant
attraper	to catch, to trap
servir	to serve
content	content or happy
accord	accord or harmony
cru	crude or raw

DRILL 3

Question	Answer	Explanation

xxxxx xxxxxxxx légumes xxxx xxxxx . . .
             vegetables
	B	(A) *cheminée*
		     chimney
		(B) ***jardin***
		     garden
		(C) *gazon*
		     lawn
		(D) *quartier*
		     quarter or neighborhood

xx xxxx xxxxxxx x *tombée* xxx xxxx . . .
             fallen
	C	(A) *envolée*
		     taken flight
		(B) *échappée*
		     escaped
		(C) ***cassée***
		     broken
		(D) *attrapée*
		     caught

xx xx x xxx xxxxx *chaises* xxxx . . . xxxx xx xxxxx.
             chairs
	B	(A) *assommer*
		     to knock out
		(B) ***s'asseoir***
		     to sit down
		(C) *assurer*
		     to assure
		(D) *associer*
		     to associate

xxxxx xxxx *ne se sent pas bien* xxxxx xxx . . .
          doesn't feel well
	A	(A) ***une fièvre***
		     a fever
		(B) *une armoire*
		     a wardrobe
		(C) *un verger*
		     an orchard
		(D) *une annonce*
		     an announcement

Question	Answer	Explanation

xx xxxxx xxxx xxxxxxxxx xxxxx *mangé* xxx xxx . . .
        eaten
	C	(A) *soutenir*
		    to support
		(B) *emporter*
		    to take or carry away
		(C) *avaler*
		    to swallow
		(D) *évaluer*
		    to evaluate

PRACTICE SECTION

Question		Answer	Key Word or Phrase	Fill In
1	It's cold outside. Are all the . . . closed?	C	*fait froid*	windows
2	Don't make any noise; the children are . . .	B	*bruit, enfants*	asleep
3	Are these flowers from your . . . ?	C	*fleurs*	garden
4	This coat lacks . . . where I can put my wallet.	C	*manteau, porte-monnaie*	pockets
5	Jeanne woke up . . . in order to see the sunrise.	D	*lever du soleil*	early
6	The train left the . . . at noon.	D	*train*	station
7	For Sunday's meal, we eat a . . . with potatoes.	A	*repas*	food
8	The tarts that are sold in this . . . are delicious.	A	*tartes*	pastry shop
9	You can wash yourself now. The bathroom is . . .	B	*salle de bains*	open, empty
10	My . . . for class is to translate a poem of Rimbaud's.	D	*classe*	homework, assignment
11	The noise in a club can be so loud that it hurts one's . . .	A	*bruit*	ears

Question		Answer	Key Word or Phrase	Fill In
12	The moon is so . . . that I cannot imagine that man has gone there.	C	*lune*	far away
13	It's not necessary to take out the garbage; Jean did it . . .	C	*l'a . . . fait*	already
14	We are spending Christmas with my grandparents . . .	C	*Noël*	winter
15	You've already done your homework? That . . .	D	*déjà*	surprises me, pleases me
16	Aren't you . . . of doing that stupid thing?	D	*bêtise*	ashamed, embarrassed
17	This fabric is . . . like the skin of a baby.	C	*peau d'un bébé*	soft
18	The fox . . . the hunters.	C	*renard, chasseurs*	escaped, was caught
19	The film starts at exactly 8 o'clock; be . . .	A	*commence*	on time, early
20	There are too many people here; I prefer cafés that are less . . .	D	*trop de monde*	crowded
21	There is not enough evidence . . . this man.	D	*pas assez de preuves*	to convict, charge, indict
22	My brother is . . . ; he never wants to help me clean the kitchen.	B	*il ne veut jamais m'aider*	lazy, selfish
23	The vase that I dropped . . .	D	*laissé tomber*	broke, shattered
24	You can find your grandmother's wedding dress if you look in . . .	B	*la robe de mariée de votre grand-mère*	the attic
25	She got rid of her . . . clothing.	C	*s'est débarrassée*	unwanted, messed up
26	Diane cut her . . . so she would be more fashionable.	C	*s'est coupé*	hair
27	To establish the validity of his theory, the scientist conducted . . .	B	*établir la validité*	an experiment, study

CHAPTER 5

DRILL 1: PRONOUN QUESTIONS

Question		Answer	Explanation
1	*------- est arrivé à Paul hier?* What happened to Paul yesterday?	D	(A) *Quel* *Quel* means "which" and is used to modify a noun (*Quelle voiture est la vôtre?*). We need something that means "what." (B) *Quoi* In questions, *quoi* is used only with a preposition (*À quoi sert cet exercice?*). (C) *Qu'* *Qu'* is a shortened form of *que*. Since the "what" of the question is the subject (what happened), it cannot be *que*. **(D) *Qu'est-ce qui* is correct. You cannot use *qui* alone because that would mean "who happened to Paul yesterday?" And you need qui here because it is directly followed by a verb.**
2	*C'est -------.* It is he.	C	With *c'est* or *ce sont* you use either a noun or a stressed pronoun. (A) *eux* *Eux* is a stressed pronoun, which is correct, but since it is plural, the correct sentence would be *Ce sont eux*. (B) *il* *Il* is a subject pronoun. No good here. (C) *lui* **Lui can be a singular stressed pronoun. This is the correct answer.** (D) *le* *Le* is a direct object pronoun. Cancel it.

Question		Answer	Explanation
3	*C'est grâce à ------- que nous avons pu venir.* It is thanks to them that we could come.	A	Because the pronoun is being used with a preposition (but not as an indirect object), we want a stressed pronoun. (A) *eux* **Eux is a stressed pronoun, so this is the correct choice.** (B) *les* *Les* is the direct object pronoun. (C) *leur* *Leur* is the indirect object pronoun. (D) *ils* *Ils* is the subject pronoun.
4	*La chose la plus difficile est de ------- réveiller le matin.* The most difficult thing is to wake him up in the morning.	C	The verb in this sentence is *réveiller*, a verb that takes a direct object. The correct answer must serve as a direct object pronoun. (A) *lui* *Lui* can be an indirect object pronoun or a stressed pronoun. (B) *il* *Il* is the subject pronoun. (C) *le* **Le is the direct object pronoun, so this is the correct answer.** (D) *moi* *Moi* is the stressed pronoun.

Question		Answer	Explanation
5	------- *a sorti la poubelle.* No one took out the garbage.	B	(A) *Il n'* This choice does not work because the sentence lacks the *pas* that must be used with *ne* (*n'*) to make a negative. (B) *Personne n'* **This is the correct answer.** *Personne* **must be used with** *ne* **and does not need the** *pas.* (C) *Aucun* Like *personne*, *aucun* must be used with *ne*. (D) *Qui* *Qui* can begin the sentence in a question, but not in a statement.

DRILL 2: VERB QUESTIONS

Question		Answer	Explanation
1	*Si* -------, *je préparerais le dîner.* If I had time, I would make dinner.	C	Since the conditional tense is used in the portion of the sentence following the blank, the verb that precedes it must be in the **imperfect**. Only choice (C) has a verb in the imperfect. (A) *vous en avez envie*—present (B) *on me le demande*—present **(C)** *j'avais le temps*—**imperfect** (D) *tu seras d'accord*—future
2	*Paul regrette que nous* ------- *pas réussi.* Paul regrets that we have not succeeded.	C	What mode is used with verbs like *regretter que*? The subjunctive. Only choice (C) has the subjunctive. (A) *n'avons*—present (B) *n'avions*—imperfect **(C)** *n'ayons*—**subjunctive (present)** (D) *n'aurons*—future

Question		Answer	Explanation
3	*------ une lettre quand on a sonné à la porte.* I was writing a letter when the doorbell rang.	D	The use of the *passé composé* indicates that the sentence takes place in the past, so you can eliminate (A), (B), and (C). The answer is (D). The use of the imperfect indicates that the action of letter writing was ongoing when the doorbell rang. (A) *J'écris*—present (B) *J'écrirais*—conditional (C) *J'écrive*—subjunctive (present) **(D) *J'écrivais*—imperfect**
4	*Elle n'a jamais oublié ce que nous ------- au moment de son départ.* She never forgot what we said at the moment of her departure.	C	Does the expression *ce que* take the subjunctive? No. Eliminate (B). The use of the *passé composé* in the first part of the sentence indicates that the sentence takes place in the past. Eliminate (A) and (D). The correct answer is (C). (A) *disons*—present (B) *ayons dit*—past of the subjunctive **(C) *avons dit*—*passé composé*** (D) *aurions dit*—past of the conditional
5	*Est-ce que vous ------- contents si je n'avais pas accepté l'invitation?* Would you have been happy if I had not accepted the invitation?	D	Since a form of the imperfect is being used with *si*, the other verb must be in the conditional. Choice (D) is the only verb in the conditional. Since one part of the sentence has the past form of the imperfect (*the plus-que-parfait*), it makes sense that the conditional verb would also be in a past form. (A) *êtes*—present (B) *soyez*—subjunctive (C) *étiez*—imperfect **(D) *auriez été*—past of the conditional**
6	*Nous doutons ------- leur rendre visite chez eux.* We doubt that he has time to visit them.	A	Does the verb *douter que* take the subjunctive? Yes, so (B), (C), and (D) must be wrong. Choice (A) is the correct answer because the subjunctive is used. **(A) *qu'il ait le temps de*—subjunctive** (B) *qu'il voudrait*—conditional (C) *qu'il peut*—present (D) *qu'elle avait envie de*—imperfect

Question		Answer	Explanation
7	*-------, elle est partie pour le long trajet chez elle.* Having said goodbye, she left for the long journey home.	C	We need a verb form that shows when she said goodbye (the verb is in all the answer choices). We can eliminate (B), since it is the infinitive and the sentence is in the past. To show that she said goodbye either before or as she left, we need either the perfect or the present participle. The only participle here is (C), the perfect participle, "having said goodbye." This is our answer. The other choices, (A) and (D), cannot be used by themselves in a phrase. (A) *Disait au revoir*—imperfect (B) *Dire au revoir*—infinitive (C) **Ayant dit au revoir—perfect participle** (D) *Avoir dit au revoir*—past infinitive
8	*Tu pourras regarder la télé une fois que tu --------- ton travail.* You will be allowed to watch TV once you have finished your homework.	C	Does the conjunction une fois que take the subjunctive? No. Eliminate (D). We need a verb form that shows that your homework must be finished in the future before you may watch TV. Choice (B) is the imperfect so it does not work. Choice (A) is the past form of the conditional, so it does not work either. The correct answer is (C), futur antérieur, future perfect tense. (A) aurais fini—past conditional (B) finissais—imperfect (C) **auras fini—future perfect** (D) finisses—subjunctive

DRILL 3: PREPOSITION QUESTIONS

Question	Answer	Explanation
1 *Marie ------- les résultats de ses examens.* Marie is waiting for the results of her exams.	B	(A) *pense* Penser requires the preposition *à* or *de*. **(B) *attend*** ***Attendre* requires no preposition. This is the correct answer.** (C) *compte* *Compter* requires the preposition *sur*. Without a preposition, it means "to count" and makes no sense here. (D) *a envie* *Avoir envie* requires the preposition *de*.
2 *Je ------- de leur écrire.* I am compelled to write them.	A	**(A) *suis obligé*** **This is the correct answer. *Être obligé* requires the preposition *de*.** (B) *espère* *Espérer* takes no preposition in French. (C) *veux* *Vouloir* takes no preposition. It cannot be used with *de*. (D) *réfléchis* *Réfléchir* takes the preposition *à*. It cannot be used with *de*.
3 *Je n'ai jamais eu l'occasion ------- voir ce film.* I have never had the opportunity to see this film.	C	The expression *avoir l'occasion* takes the preposition *de*. **(C) is the correct answer.**

Question		Answer	Explanation
4	*------- le concert, elles bavardaient sans cesse.* During the concert, they chattered endlessly.	A	(A) *Pendant* ***Pendant* means "during." This is the correct answer.** (B) *Dans* *Dans* means "in." You cannot say *dans le concert*. (C) *Avec* *Avec* means "with." You might find a context in which *avec* works with *le concert*, but in this context, it does not. (D) *En* There might be a context in which *en concert* is acceptable, but *en le concert* is never correct.
5	*Je la vois souvent à -------.* I see her often at the bakery.	C	(A) *France* The correct expression would be *en France*. (B) *ville* You can say either *à la ville* or *en ville*. **(C) *la boulangerie*** **This is the correct answer. You can say *à la boulangerie*.** (D) *loin* *Loin* is never used with *à*.
6	*Elle n'a pas réfléchi ------- de refuser l'offre.* She did not think before refusing the offer.	B	(A) --- *Réfléchir* must be used with a preposition. **(B) *avant*** **This is the correct answer.** (C) *après* You cannot say *après de*. *Après* is used with the infinitive (e.g., *après avoir réfléchi*). (D) *à* You cannot have these two prepositions, *à* and *de*, following each other.

PRACTICE SECTION

Part B

Question	Category	Answer	Explanation
1	Odds and Ends	A	**(A)** *quelque chose* **is correct** (B) *rien* must be used with *ne—n'a rien* (C) *plusieurs* must modify something (D) *quelque* must modify something
2	Prepositions	C	(A) *rejeter* cannot be followed by a verb (B) *aimer* takes the infinitive **(C)** *être obligé* **takes** *de*, **so it is correct** (D) *avoir voulu* takes the infinitive
3	Odds and Ends	B	(A) plural **(B)** *amie* **is feminine, but it's correct because** *amie* **begins with a vowel** (C) feminine (D) plural
4	Odds and Ends	A	**(A)** *avant de partir* **works with the future tense** (B) *tout à l'heure* is okay, but not with *à* (C) *hier* does not work with the future (D) *jamais* must be used with *ne*
5	Pronouns	D	(A) *personne* requires *ne* (B) subject pronoun (C) indirect object **(D) stressed pronoun is correct with** *c'est*
6	Prepositions	A	**(A)** *préférer* **takes the infinitive—correct** (B) *rêver* takes *de* and then the infinitive (C) *plaire* takes no direct object (D) *insister* takes *pour* and the infinitive
7	Pronouns	D	(A) subject or stressed pronoun (B) stressed pronoun (C) reflexive, but wrong person **(D)** *demander quelque chose à quelqu'un*—**indirect object is correct**

Question	Category	Answer	Explanation
8	Pronouns	C	(A) indirect object pronoun (B) subject pronoun **(C) stressed pronoun is correct with *avec*** (D) direct object pronoun
9	Pronouns	B	(A) plural **(B) singular and feminine possessive pronoun—correct** (C) *aucun* requires *ne* (D) possessive adjective
10	Prepositions	A	**(A) *Russie* is feminine—correct with *en*** (B) *États-Unis* is plural (*aux*) (C) New York takes *à* (D) Canada is masculine (*au*)
11	Odds and Ends	C	(A) adverb (B) adverb **(C) adjective—correct** (D) preposition
12	Verbs	B	(A) *savoir que* doesn't take the subjunctive **(B) *regretter que* takes the subjunctive—correct** (C) *oublier que* doesn't take the subjunctive (D) nothing hypothetical, so no subjunctive
13	Pronouns/Prepositions	A	**(A) *parler* takes *de*—therefore *dont* is correct** (B) *quoi* is used with things (C) *parler* cannot work with *sauf* (D) *avant que* is a conjunction, not a pronoun
14	Pronouns	C	(A) *quelle* is feminine (B) *qu'est-ce qui* is used to refer to things **(C) *Où* means "where"—correct** (D) *quoi* is used with things
15	Pronouns	D	(A) *quel* must modify something (B) *y* refers to place or location (C) *dont* cannot be used to begin a question **(D) *avoir envie* takes *de*—correct**

Question	Category	Answer	Explanation
16	Prepositions	C	(A) *aller* does not take *de* (B) *espérer* takes either the infinitive or *que* **(C) *essayer* takes *de*—correct** (D) *pouvoir* does not take *de*
17	Verbs	C	(A) *sans doute* means "probably" (B) certain, so no subjunctive **(C) *Je crains* means "I fear." This expression takes the subjunctive—correct** (D) no doubt or uncertainty, so no subjunctive
18	Prepositions	C	(A) in order to (B) when **(C) in spite of—correct** (D) unless
19	Verbs	A	**(A) imperfect followed by conditional—correct** (B) present, so following clause can't be conditional (C) future cannot follow *si* (D) past imperfect would take past conditional
20	Verbs	D	(A) *passé composé* (B) *passé composé* (C) *passé composé* **(D) subjunctive is used with superlatives—correct**

Part C

Question	Category	Answer	Explanation
21	Verbs	D	(A) imperfect (B) past imperfect (C) present **(D) past conditional follows a clause with *si* and the past imperfect—correct**
22	Pronouns	B	(A) subject or stressed pronoun **(B) indirect object—correct** (C) stressed pronoun and masculine (D) direct object and singular

Question	Category	Answer	Explanation
23	Pronouns	A	**(A) stressed pronoun with *chez*—correct** (B) subject (C) indirect object (D) subject and masculine
24	Vocabulary	A	**(A) no one—correct** (B) a person (C) nothing (D) *nulle* is an adjective
25	Vocabulary	A	**(A) Finally—correct** (B) *Terminé* is not an adverb, but a past participle (C) Now (D) In order to
26	Pronouns	B	(A) *arriver de* makes no sense in this context **(B) *y* indicates place: in this case, the café—correct** (C) *le* is a direct object pronoun (D) *arriver* cannot be reflexive
27	Verbs	D	(A) no agreement or masculine singular (B) feminine singular (C) masculine plural **(D) feminine plural: requires agreement because direct object precedes verb—correct**
28	Prepositions	B	(A) *cinéma* is masculine **(B) *au* is correct because *cinéma* is masculine** (C) *entrer par* doesn't make sense in this context and *cinéma* is masculine (D) *entrer par* doesn't make sense in this context
29	Prepositions	C	(A) you cannot use *avant* and a verb without a preposition (B) *avant à* does not exist **(C) the correct expression is *avant de*** (D) *avant que* would have to be followed by a clause using the subjunctive
30	Verbs	A	**(A) no agreement required—correct** (B) feminine (C) masculine plural (D) feminine plural

Question	Category	Answer	Explanation
31	Prepositions	D	(A) needs a preposition to make sense (B) *à demander* makes no sense (C) *de demander* makes no sense (D) *pour demander*: **to ask—correct**
32	Conjunctions	A	(A) *si*—**correct** (B) when (C) which (D) who
33	Vocabulary	C	(A) *en temps* does not exist; *à temps* (on time) would be correct (B) every hour (C) **on time—correct** (D) from time to time

CHAPTER 6

PRACTICE SECTION

Question		Answer	Explanation
1	Etienne lacked the energy to	B	(A) "sleep": familiar word—wrong context (B) **"undress": see phrase *tout vêtu* (fully dressed)** (C) "eat" (D) "put on his clothes"
2	According to the passage, why is Etienne tired?	D	(A) "He ate too much." familiar words—wrong context (B) "He did not sleep at all in two days." Too extreme; he did get some sleep. (C) "He went to sleep at four in the morning." familiar words—wrong context (D) **"He has slept only for a few hours in 48 hours": see *En deux jours, il n'avait pas dormi quatre heures.***

Question		Answer	Explanation
3	At what time of day did he get up?	C	(A) "early in the morning" (B) "noon" (C) **"early in the evening"**: see *au crépuscule, avant de . . . se coucher pour la nuit* (D) "midnight"
4	How does he react at the moment he wakes up?	A	(A) **"He doesn't remember where he is"**: see *sans reconnaître le lieu où il se trouvait* (B) "He can't find his clothes." (C) "He feels that he is late." (D) "He is hungry."
5	What did he want to do before eating dinner?	B	(A) "breathe" (B) **"go for a walk"**: see *prendre l'air* (C) "wake up": familiar words—wrong context (D) "run"
6	When did Morissot leave to reach the island?	C	(A) "after sunset" (B) "at sunset" (C) **"at sunrise"**: see *dès l'aurore* (D) "in the afternoon"
7	How did he reach the island?	D	(A) "by bus and on foot" (B) "by boat" (C) "by car and on foot" (D) **"by train and on foot"**: see *chemin de fer* (railway), *à pied*
8	At what point did he start fishing?	A	(A) **"at almost the moment he arrived"**: see *à peine arrivé* (B) "at the moment he started to dream" (C) "at nightfall" (D) "when his friend arrived"
9	What is located on Notre-Dame-de-Lorette Street?	C	(A) "the island": makes no sense (B) "the place the two friends would meet" (C) **"Mr. Savage's shop"**: see *mercier* (dealer in sewing wares) (D) "the train station"

Question		Answer	Explanation
10	The parents of Guillaume	D	(A) "advise him never to go to the movies" (B) "don't concern themselves with what he does" (C) "don't like the movies" **(D) "give their opinion about the films he chooses": see *je leur demande ce qu'ils en pensent***
11	To Gilles's question, Claire replies	C	(A) "that she never goes to the movies" (B) "that she goes to the movies if her parents agree" **(C) "that she goes to the movies without telling her parents": see *en cachette* (secretly)** (D) "that she goes to the movies often"
12	What reason does Guillaume give for not lying to his parents?	B	(A) "His parents let him do anything.": familiar words—wrong context **(B) "His parents let him decide what to do.": see *Je crois que je me sens libre*** (C) "It is better not to do it." (D) "His parents don't like the movies."
13	The author reacts to the change in Boulevard St. Michel and Place Saint-André-des-Arts with	B	(A) "impatience" **(B) "regret"** (C) "indifference" (D) "pleasure": makes no sense
14	What does one find near Luxembourg?	D	(A) "small, anonymous restaurants": familiar words—wrong context (B) "pleasant cafés": familiar words—wrong context (C) "pretentious bookstores" **(D) "American establishments": *McDonald's***
15	According to the passage, "Gibert" is	C	(A) "a film" (B) "a café" **(C) "a bookstore": see *cinémas et librairies semblent résister*** (D) "a museum"

Question		Answer	Explanation
16	What do young people do instead of going to Boulevard St. Michel?	C	(A) "They go to Place Saint-André-des-Arts." (B) "They are in a rush to see American films." **(C) "They look for cool bars in another area.":** see *autour du Panthéon* (D) "They resist going to bookstores."
17	The narrator lets it be understood that she	D	(A) "worked a lot" (B) "was an invalid" (C) "had many worries" **(D) "married her father's friend":** see *Un vieil ami de mon père m'a demandé ma main.*
18	The brother of the narrator	B	(A) "lived with her for six years": familiar words—wrong context **(B) "was younger than she":** *cadet* (C) "was a soldier" (D) "didn't like her husband"
19	The passage gives us the impression	A	**(A) "that she wanted to defend her actions":** see *Qu'auriez-vous fait à ma place?* (B) "that she missed her husband" (C) "that her brother was cured" (D) "that she liked good weather": misunderstanding, as *sans un nuage* is not literal
20	After six years, what happened?	D	(A) "The husband of the narrator left." (B) "The good weather changed.": *sans un nuage* is not literal (C) "The narrator decided to leave." **(D) "The narrator found a lover.":** see *j'ai rencontré celui que je devais aimer.*
21	It is understood that Antoine Lemurier	D	(A) "is dead" (B) "missed the train" (C) "left his work" **(D) "nearly succumbed to an illness":** see *avait manqué mourir* (almost died)

Question		Answer	Explanation
22	What did the neighbors think of Lemurier's illness?	A	(A) "They expected an interesting end to the tragedy.": see *ils vivaient anxieusement dans l'attente d'un dénouement qui fût digne de la pièce* (B) "They were sad." (C) "They were angry with Lemurier." (D) "They fell ill."
23	According to the neighbors, what would have been a fitting end to the situation?	C	(A) "Mr. Lemurier loses his job." (B) "Mr. Lemurier completely recovers." (C) "Mrs. Lemurier is without shelter.": see *la femme à la rue* (D) "Mrs. Lemurier sells the house.": close, but the phrase is *le mobilier être vendu*

Part IV
The Princeton Review
Practice SAT French Subject
Tests and Explanations

Chapter 9
Practice SAT French
Subject Test 1

FRENCH SUBJECT TEST 1

SECTION 1

Your responses to the SAT French questions must be filled in on Section 1 of your answer sheet (at the back of the book). Marks on any other section will not be counted toward your score.

When your supervisor gives the signal, turn the page and begin the SAT French Subject Test.

FRENCH SUBJECT TEST 1

PLEASE NOTE THAT YOUR ANSWER SHEET HAS FIVE ANSWER POSITIONS, MARKED A, B, C, D, E, WHILE THE QUESTIONS THROUGHOUT THIS TEST CONTAIN ONLY FOUR CHOICES. BE SURE <u>NOT</u> TO MAKE ANY MARKS IN COLUMN E.

Part A

Directions: This part consists of a number of incomplete statements, each having four suggested completions. Select the most appropriate completion and fill in the corresponding oval on the answer sheet.

1. Je dois faire ma . . . avant de partir en vacances demain.

   (A) bouche
   (B) voiture
   (C) valise
   (D) faute

2. Il fait beau <u>dehors</u>; veux-tu te . . . après le dîner?

   (A) laver
   (B) demander
   (C) lever
   (D) promener

3. Le soldat attendait avec impatience la fin de . . .

   (A) la route
   (B) la gare
   (C) la guerre
   (D) l'immeuble

4. Il est interdit de garder vos chaussures dans la maison; laissez-les . . .

   (A) de plus
   (B) d'accord
   (C) d'habitude
   (D) dehors

5. Paul a besoin d' . . . pour soutenir son pantalon.

   (A) un bras
   (B) une poche
   (C) une jambe
   (D) une ceinture

6. Pour son anniversaire, le garçon a reçu plusieurs . . .

   (A) jours
   (B) talents
   (C) jardins
   (D) cadeaux

7. J'ai acheté . . . dans la boulangerie d'à côté.

   (A) des fruits
   (B) du pain
   (C) de la viande
   (D) du boulot

8. Le . . . de mon immeuble est 564.

   (A) nombre
   (B) guide
   (C) numéro
   (D) nom

GO ON TO THE NEXT PAGE

9. Il y a douze . . . dans un an.
   (A) mois
   (B) jours
   (C) heures
   (D) saisons

10. Le cinéma est vide; nous pouvons nous . . . n'importe où.
    (A) endormir
    (B) articuler
    (C) assister
    (D) asseoir

11. Quand je porte mes souliers préférés, je n'ai jamais mal aux . . .
    (A) coudes
    (B) pieds
    (C) lèvres
    (D) oreilles

12. Je suis d'accord avec lui; je pense qu'il a . . .
    (A) tort
    (B) raison
    (C) mal
    (D) nécessité

    avoir raison

13. Mon bureau se trouve dans un . . . différent de mon appartement.
    (A) quartier
    (B) gazon
    (C) voyage
    (D) plan

14. Le héros a . . . une fille qui était en train de se noyer.
    (A) sauvé
    (B) nagé
    (C) remercié
    (D) traîné

15. L'été, il faut porter des . . . de soleil pour se protéger les yeux.
    (A) spectacles
    (B) cheveux
    (C) lunettes
    (D) rayons

16. Il faut faire attention avant de . . . la rue.
    (A) traverser
    (B) transpirer
    (C) traduire
    (D) transformer

GO ON TO THE NEXT PAGE

17. Ce n'est pas gentil de . . . tes amis.

    (A) lire
    (B) remplir
    (C) taquiner
    (D) tolérer

18. Le bruit constant m'. . .

    (A) énerve
    (B) enseigne
    (C) enlève
    (D) enferme

19. Le serveur a . . . mon verre de vin.

    (A) rempli
    (B) reculé
    (C) remonté
    (D) revu

20. La dame a . . . le bras pour attraper le ballon.

    (A) tendu
    (B) renversé
    (C) retiré
    (D) perdu

21. L'étudiant a écrit . . . sur les oeuvres de Maupassant.

    (A) une boulette
    (B) une recette
    (C) une dissertation
    (D) un témoin

22. Sans la protection d'un parapluie, je vais être . . . par la pluie.

    (A) tenté
    (B) trempé
    (C) tendu
    (D) tempéré

GO ON TO THE NEXT PAGE

Part B

Directions: Each of the following sentences contains a blank. From the four choices given, select the one that can be inserted in the blank to form a grammatically correct sentence and fill in the corresponding oval on the answer sheet. Choice (A) may consist of dashes that indicate that no insertion is required to form a grammatically correct sentence.

23. Le monsieur ------- à vous suggérer.

    (A) n'a quelque chose
    (B) n'a pas
    (C) n'a rien
    (D) a rien

24. À ------- <u>est</u> ce manteau vert?

    (A) que
    (B) qui
    (C) lequel
    (D) quoi

25. J'aime beaucoup cet -------.

    (A) homme
    (B) huile d'olive
    (C) dame
    (D) livre

26. Aimez-vous la plage? Nous ------- allons après la classe.

    (A) en
    (B) où
    (C) y
    (D) là

27. La semaine prochaine je visite ma cousine à -------.

    (A) Mexique
    (B) France
    (C) Paris
    (D) Chine

se plaindre de

28. ------- vous vous <u>plaignez</u> est incroyable.

    (A) De quoi
    (B) Ce que
    (C) Ce dont
    (D) A quoi

29. Jean-Claude est venu avec -------.

    (A) ils
    (B) leur
    (C) eux
    (D) soi

à

30. C'est une décision ------- <u>laquelle</u> je vais beaucoup réfléchir.

    (A) à
    (B) sans
    (C) avec
    (D) dont

31. C'est lui qui ------- vendu la voiture.

    (A) a
    (B) est
    (C) aie
    (D) soit

32. Il a appris la nouvelle au moment ------- il a allumé la télé.

    (A) quand
    (B) aprés
    (C) où — *used*
    (D) durant

GO ON TO THE NEXT PAGE

33. Pierre ------- dehors quand le téléphone a sonné.

    (A) est
    (B) était
    (C) soit
    (D) serait

34. Si Paul achetait un journal, il ------- déjà les résultats.

    (A) savait
    (B) aurait su
    (C) saura
    (D) saurait

35. ------- les mains avant de manger!

    (A) Lavez
    (B) Brossez-vous
    (C) Serrez
    (D) Lavez-vous

36. Il n'a pas ------- signer les papiers.

    (A) décidé
    (B) le droit
    (C) envie
    (D) voulu

37. Il faut que tu ------- attention avant de traverser la rue.

    (A) fasses
    (B) fais
    (C) feras
    (D) faisais

38. C'est à cause de ------- que nous avons raté le train.

    (A) il
    (B) moi
    (C) se
    (D) leur

39. Est-ce que ------- cette dame qui va nous montrer la chambre?

    (A) c'est
    (B) ce soit
    (C) c'était
    (D) sera

40. Mon travail est ------- que le vôtre.

    (A) si difficile
    (B) le meilleur
    (C) pire
    (D) trop

41. Nous avons beaucoup progressé ------- l'époque du Professeur LeBlanc.

    (A) durant
    (B) sinon
    (C) afin de
    (D) avant que

42. ------- m'a écrit.

    (A) Celui qui
    (B) Tu
    (C) C'est lui qui
    (D) Personne

GO ON TO THE NEXT PAGE

Part C

Directions: The paragraphs below contain blank spaces indicating omissions in the text. For some blanks, it is necessary to choose the completion that is most appropriate to the meaning of the passage; for other blanks, to choose the one completion that forms a grammatically correct sentence. In some instances, choice (A) may consist of dashes that indicate that no insertion is required to form a grammatically correct sentence. In each case, indicate your answer by filling in the corresponding oval on the answer sheet. Be sure to read the paragraph completely before answering the questions related to it.

Il est trois heures et demie du matin quand j' ----(43)---- avec ma femme, sur le terrain de l'aérodrome pour le grand départ. Après avoir ----(44)---- pendant plusieurs jours un temps ----(45)----, nous sommes ----(46)---- prêts à partir ----(47)---- Tokyo. My femme, qui ----(48)---- née ----(49)---- Japon, n'a ----(50)---- visité la capitale, Tokyo. Elle voilait ----(51)---- y aller.

43. (A) arrivais
    (B) arriverais
    (C) arrive
    (D) étais arrivé

44. (A) attendu
    (B) attendue
    (C) attendus
    (D) attendues

45. (A) passé
    (B) jamais
    (C) enfin
    (D) simplement

46. (A) loin d'être
    (B) mauvais
    (C) triste
    (D) favorable

47. (A) dans
    (B) sans
    (C) en
    (D) pour

48. (A) était
    (B) soit
    (C) est
    (D) es

49. (A) en
    (B) au
    (C) à
    (D) dans

50. (A) encore
    (B) pas encore
    (C) jamais
    (D) guère

51. (A) souvent
    (B) parfois
    (C) simplement
    (D) tellement

GO ON TO THE NEXT PAGE

Trois ou quatre cents personnes sont là pour ----(52)---- à notre envol. Je ne sais pas comment cela se fait, ----(53)---- que nous n'avions dit à personne que nous partions. Je suis très ----(54)----, mais notre avion est très chargé et la piste est couverte d'herbe. Je connais bien les dangers qu'il y a à ----(55)---- dans ces conditions. Tout a été longuement ----(56)----, discuté entre nous depuis des ----(57)----, avec une très grande attention. Maintenant, j' ----(58)---- l'esprit tranquille.

52. (A) assister
    (B) assommer
    (C) asseoir
    (D) aspirer

53. (A) malgré
    (B) parce
    (C) sans
    (D) dès

54. (A) fière
    (B) énervé
    (C) calme
    (D) lourd

55. (A) débarrasser
    (B) déborder
    (C) développer
    (D) décoller

56. (A) étudié
    (B) étudier
    (C) étude
    (D) étudiant

57. (A) minutes
    (B) secondes
    (C) moments
    (D) semaines

58. (A) ai
    (B) avais
    (C) aurais
    (D) ai été

GO ON TO THE NEXT PAGE

Part D

Directions: Read the following texts carefully for comprehension. Each is followed by a number of questions or incomplete statements. Select the completion or answer that is best according to the text and fill in the corresponding oval on the answer sheet.

Ayant laissé la voiture au garage, ils décidèrent d'attendre dans un café. Les longues files de maisons qui s'étendaient de chaque côté de la route ne formaient
Ligne pas un village. C'était plutôt comme un faubourg lointain
5 de Chartres, avec des maisons basses, et çà et là une devanture terne d'épicerie de campagne. Deux enfants couraient l'un après l'autre. On entendait quelqu'un frapper régulièrement une pièce de métal dans un atelier voisin. Ils se dirigèrent vers le café le plus proche.
10 C'était l'heure creuse. Il n'y avait personne. Un chat dormait sur le comptoir. Le patron apparut au bout de quelques instants, comme à regret, en traînant les jambes. Ils commandèrent n'importe quoi pour justifier leur présence. Pendant qu'il les servait, elle avait tiré
15 un poudrier de son sac et vérifiait son maquillage, machinalement. Elle était engourdie, un peu dolente, comme si on l'eût enveloppée dans une couche épaisse de coton, et les bruits ne lui parvenaient qu'assourdis. Peut-être la fatigue du voyage.
(Jean Forgère, *La Panne,* Le Livre de Poche)

59. Qu'est-ce que le couple a fait avant de chercher le café?

    (A) Ils ont attendu.
    (B) Ils ont emmené leur automobile à un garage.
    (C) Ils ont parlé avec deux enfants.
    (D) Ils ont frappé quelque chose.

60. Où se trouve le couple?

    (A) À Chartres
    (B) Dans un village
    (C) Dans une grande ville
    (D) Dans la banlieue d'une ville

61. Quelle est la raison pour laquelle le couple est venu au café?

    (A) Pour manger un bon repas
    (B) Pour trouver quelqu'un avec qui ils pourraient parler
    (C) Pour demander leur chemin — route
    (D) Pour passer le temps

62. Qu'est-ce que l'auteur veut dire par l'expression "l'heure creuse"?

    (A) Qu'il y avait beaucoup de monde dans le café
    (B) Qu'il faisait presque nuit
    (C) Que personne n'était là
    (D) Que c'était l'heure où le café fermait

63. Quelle impression avait la dame au café?

    (A) Qu'elle avait mangé du coton
    (B) Qu'elle était trop maquillée
    (C) Qu'il y avait trop de bruit
    (D) Qu'elle entendait mal

GO ON TO THE NEXT PAGE

Il y a, au fond de beaucoup de Français, un champion de course automobile qui sommeille et que réveille le simple contact du pied sur l'accélérateur. Le citoyen
Ligne paisible, qui vous a obligeamment invité à prendre place
5 dans sa voiture, peut se métamorphoser sous vos yeux en pilote démoniaque. Jérôme Charnelet, ce bon père de famille, qui n'écraserait pas une mouche contre une vitre, est tout prêt à écraser un piéton au kilomètre, pourvu qu'il se sente "dans son droit." Au signal vert, il voit rouge.
10 Rien ne l'arrête plus, pas même le jaune. Sur la route, cet homme, qui passe pour rangé, ne se range pas du tout. Ce n'est qu'à bout de ressources, et après avoir subi une klaxonnade nourrie, qu'il consentira de mauvaise grâce à abandonner le milieu de la chaussée.
(*L'Auto,* Hachette)

64. L'auteur écrit dans un style

(A) sérieux
(B) neutre
(C) drôle
(D) scientifique

65. Qu'est-ce qui fait apparaître le "champion de course automobile"?

(A) L'action de se mettre au volant de l'automobile
(B) Le lever du soleil
(C) L'action de se réveiller
(D) Un klaxon

66. D'après le passage, Jérôme Charnelet est d'habitude

(A) un champion de course
(B) d'une disposition aimable
(C) impatient
(D) généreux

67. Comment Jérôme réagit-il au signal vert?

(A) Il s'arrête.
(B) Il écrase une mouche.
(C) Il ne réussit pas à voir les couleurs.
(D) Il devient un conducteur démoniaque.

68. D'après le passage, qu'est-ce qui convaincrait Jérôme de changer de position sur la chaussée?

(A) La réalisation qu'il est au milieu de la route
(B) Son sens de ses obligations envers les autres conducteurs
(C) Les klaxons des autres conducteurs
(D) La couleur du signal

69. On comprend que Jérôme conduit d'une manière

(A) ordonnée
(B) rangée
(C) gracieuse
(D) obsédée

GO ON TO THE NEXT PAGE

92 HAUTS DE SEINE
Le confort du neuf, le charme de l'ancien

Résidence "Le Valvert." Aux portes de Paris et près d'un accès autoroutier, dans immeuble du XIXe siècle, 10 appartements en cours de rénovation (du studio au 4 pièces). Parking privé dans cour intérieure. Proche du centre ville avec vue exceptionnelle sur parc aux arbres centenaires.

Prix à partir de 110000

Livraison 3ème trimestre 2005.

Bureau de vente et appartement-témoin:
01 587 45 35 12

Du lundi au samedi de 9 h 30 à 19 h, le dimanche uniquement sur rendez-vous.

70. Ces appartements

    (A) vont être rénovés en 2005
    (B) ont été rénovés au XIXe siècle
    (C) sont en train d'être rénovés
    (D) sont rénovés

71. Cette publicité s'adresse à

    (A) des acheteurs éventuels
    (B) de futurs locataires
    (C) des personnes âgées
    (D) des vendeurs

72. Après avoir lu cette publicité, on connaît tout SAUF

    (A) la proximité de Paris de la résidence
    (B) les heures d'ouverture du bureau de vente
    (C) l'adresse exacte de la résidence
    (D) l'existence d'un appartement modèle

GO ON TO THE NEXT PAGE

En mars 1973, un journal parisien a demandé à des jeunes de 14-15 ans quel était, pour eux, le plus mauvais moment de la journée; plus de la moitié (57%) ont _{Ligne} répondu: "Quand je pars le matin pour l'école" et 23% ⁵ "le temps que je passe à l'école." Tout le monde aussi le sait: beaucoup de lycéens s'ennuient; ils en ont assez, ils en ont "ras le bol." Ce sont des mots qu'on entend et qu'on lit souvent. Certains disent: "Les examens, ça sert à trouver du travail, à avoir un beau métier. Sans ¹⁰ diplôme, on ne trouve rien." Mais d'autres pensent que l'école ne sert à rien, qu'ils apprennent plus de choses à la radio, au cinéma, à la télévision ou en voyageant; et aussi que l'école est souvent coupée de la vie et qu'elle est construite, comme la société, avec des chefs, une trop ¹⁵ grande hiérarchie.

(*Les Jeunes Aujourd'hui,* Hachette)

73. Ce passage concerne

(A) le nombre d'étudiants dans le système éducatif
(B) les attitudes des adolescents français
(C) le moyen de changer l'attitude des lycéens
(D) des changements récents dans le système éducatif

74. Que veut dire l'expression "ils en ont ras le bol"?

(A) Qu'ils n'ont pas assez à manger
(B) Qu'ils se plaignent des études
(C) Qu'ils doivent se raser
(D) Qu'ils ne veulent plus de quelque chose

75. D'après l'avis de certains étudiants, où est-ce qu'on apprend le plus?

(A) En famille
(B) À l'école
(C) Dans une hiérarchie
(D) Dans la vie

76. Selon les étudiants qui n'aiment pas l'école, quelle est la critique la plus forte contre le système d'éducation courant?

(A) Il y a trop de travail.
(B) Les étudiants s'ennuient.
(C) Les études n'ont rien à voir avec la vie.
(D) Il n'y a pas assez de chefs.

GO ON TO THE NEXT PAGE

Peu après, le patron m'a fait appeler et, sur le moment, j'ai été ennuyé parce que j'ai pensé qu'il allait me dire de moins téléphoner et de mieux travailler. Ce n'était pas cela du tout. Il m'a déclaré qu'il allait me parler d'un projet encore très vague. Il voulait seulement avoir mon avis sur la question. Il avait l'intention d'installer un bureau à Paris qui traiterait ses affaires sur la place, et directement, avec les grandes compagnies et il voulait savoir si j'étais disposé à y aller. Cela me permettrait de vivre à Paris et aussi de voyager une partie de l'année. "Vous êtes jeune, et il me semble que c'est une vie qui doit vous plaire." J'ai dit que oui mais que dans le fond cela m'était égal.
(Camus, *L'Étranger,* Folio)

Ligne appears at line 3, and *5* at line 5, and *10* at line 10 in the left margin.

77. Le narrateur s'attend à

   (A) être grondé par son patron
   (B) recevoir une augmentation de salaire
   (C) discuter un projet avec le patron
   (D) ennuyer le patron

78. Que fait le patron?

   (A) Il ennuie le narrateur.
   (B) Il lui commande d'aller à Paris.
   (C) Il demande ce que pense le narrateur d'une suggestion.
   (D) Il refuse de laisser aller le narrateur à Paris.

79. Que veut faire le patron à Paris?

   (A) Il veut y habiter.
   (B) Il veut travailler pour une grande compagnie.
   (C) Il veut ouvrir un bureau.
   (D) Il veut trahir sa compagnie.

80. Selon le passage, pour quelle raison le patron a-t-il suggéré le projet au narrateur?

   (A) Parce que le narrateur ne travaille pas bien
   (B) Parce que le patron pense que le narrateur serait content de cette vie
   (C) Parce que le patron est trop jeune pour le faire lui-même
   (D) Parce que tout est égal au narrateur

81. Quelle est la réaction du narrateur à l'idée d'aller à Paris?

   (A) Il est énervé.
   (B) Il est content.
   (C) Il se sent rajeuni.
   (D) Il ne s'y intéresse pas beaucoup.

GO ON TO THE NEXT PAGE

Quand une rivière est bouchée par une grosse pierre, elle attend, grossit, grossit encore. Et tout à coup la pierre saute, et l'eau, enfin libre, peut continuer son chemin. Il
Ligne se passe souvent la même chose dans l'histoire des arts.
5 Charles Trenet a fait sauter ce qui bouchait la chanson française, il a fait d'elle un art mais lui a donné, en même temps, une très grande liberté, liberté dans la musique, dans les paroles, et aussi dans les gestes du chanteur sur la scène. Après Trenet, il n'y a plus une chanson, il y a dix,
10 vingt, cent chansons: après lui les artistes se sentent plus libres de faire, d'écrire, de chanter, ce qu'ils veulent.
(*La Chanson Française Aujourd'hui,* Hachette)

82. Selon le passage, qu'est-ce qui rend une rivière plus grosse?

    (A) L'augmentation de l'eau qui sort de la bouche de la rivière
    (B) La présence de quelque chose qui bloque le chemin
    (C) La présence de pierres
    (D) La liberté de l'eau

83. Pourquoi l'auteur décrit-il une rivière?

    (A) Pour caractériser la musique de Trenet
    (B) Pour expliquer la nature
    (C) Pour montrer l'importance de Trenet
    (D) Pour faire une analogie avec le développement de la chanson

84. D'après ce passage, on comprend qu'avant Trenet la chanson

    (A) était plus comme une rivière
    (B) était plus compliquée
    (C) avait moins de possibilités
    (D) était plus artistique

85. On comprend que Trenet

    (A) a introduit une nouvelle façon de présenter une chanson
    (B) aimait beaucoup la nature
    (C) a écrit cent chansons
    (D) n'était pas aimé par les autres chanteurs

STOP
IF YOU FINISH BEFORE TIME IS CALLED, YOU MAY CHECK YOUR WORK ON THIS TEST ONLY.
DO NOT WORK ON ANY OTHER TEST IN THIS BOOK.

HOW TO SCORE THE PRINCETON REVIEW
FRENCH SUBJECT TEST

When you take the real exam, the proctors will collect your test booklet and answer sheet and send your answer sheet to New Jersey where a computer looks at the pattern of filled-in ovals on your answer sheet and gives you a score. We are providing you, however, with this more primitive way of scoring your exam.

Determining Your Score

STEP 1   Using the answers on the next page, determine how many questions you got right and how many you got wrong on the test. Remember, questions that you do not answer do not count as either right answers or wrong answers.

STEP 2   Write the number of correct answers on line A.

(A) _____

STEP 3   Write the number of wrong answers on line B. Divide that number by 3.

(B) _____ ÷ 3 = _____

STEP 4   Subtract the number of wrong answers divided by 3 on line B from the number of correct answers on line A, and round to the nearest whole number. (C) is your **raw score.**

(A) _____ − (B) _____ = (C) _____

STEP 5   To determine your **real score**, look up your raw score in the left column of the Score Conversion Table on page 183; the corresponding score on the right is the score you earned on the exam.

ANSWERS TO FRENCH SUBJECT TEST 1

Question number	Correct answer	Right	Wrong	Question number	Correct answer	Right	Wrong	Question number	Correct answer	Right	Wrong
1.	C	____	____	36.	D	____	____	71.	A	____	____
2.	D	____	____	37.	A	____	____	72.	C	____	____
3.	C	____	____	38.	B	____	____	73.	B	____	____
4.	D	____	____	39.	A	____	____	74.	D	____	____
5.	D	____	____	40.	C	____	____	75.	D	____	____
6.	D	____	____	41.	A	____	____	76.	C	____	____
7.	B	____	____	42.	C	____	____	77.	A	____	____
8.	C	____	____	43.	C	____	____	78.	C	____	____
9.	A	____	____	44.	A	____	____	79.	C	____	____
10.	D	____	____	45.	D	____	____	80.	B	____	____
11.	B	____	____	46.	C	____	____	81.	D	____	____
12.	B	____	____	47.	D	____	____	82.	B	____	____
13.	A	____	____	48.	C	____	____	83.	D	____	____
14.	A	____	____	49.	B	____	____	84.	C	____	____
15.	C	____	____	50.	C	____	____	85.	A	____	____
16.	A	____	____	51.	D	____	____				
17.	C	____	____	52.	A	____	____				
18.	A	____	____	53.	B	____	____				
19.	A	____	____	54.	C	____	____				
20.	A	____	____	55.	D	____	____				
21.	C	____	____	56.	A	____	____				
22.	B	____	____	57.	D	____	____				
23.	C	____	____	58.	A	____	____				
24.	B	____	____	59.	B	____	____				
25.	A	____	____	60.	D	____	____				
26.	C	____	____	61.	D	____	____				
27.	C	____	____	62.	C	____	____				
28.	C	____	____	63.	D	____	____				
29.	C	____	____	64.	C	____	____				
30.	A	____	____	65.	A	____	____				
31.	A	____	____	66.	B	____	____				
32.	C	____	____	67.	D	____	____				
33.	B	____	____	68.	C	____	____				
34.	D	____	____	69.	D	____	____				
35.	D	____	____	70.	C	____	____				

THE PRINCETON REVIEW FRENCH SUBJECT TEST
SCORE CONVERSION TABLE

Raw score	Scaled score	Raw score	Scaled score	Raw score	Scaled score
85	800	45	630	5	410
84	800	44	620	4	410
83	800	43	620	3	400
82	800	42	610	2	400
81	800	41	610	1	390
80	800	40	600	0	390
79	800	39	600	−1	380
78	800	38	590	−2	380
77	800	37	580	−3	370
76	790	36	580	−4	360
75	790	35	570	−5	360
74	780	34	570	−6	350
73	780	33	560	−7	350
72	770	32	560	−8	340
71	770	31	550	−9	340
70	760	30	550	−10	330
69	760	29	540	−11	330
68	750	28	540	−12	320
67	740	27	530	−13	320
66	740	26	530	−14	310
65	730	25	520	−15	300
64	730	24	520	−16	290
63	720	23	510	−17	290
62	720	22	500	−18	280
61	710	21	500	−19	280
60	710	20	490	−20	270
59	700	19	490	−21	270
58	700	18	480	−22	260
57	690	17	480	−23	260
56	690	16	470	−24	250
55	680	15	470	−25 through −28	240
54	680	14	460		
53	670	13	460		
52	660	12	450		
51	660	11	450		
50	650	10	440		
49	650	9	430		
48	640	8	430		
47	640	7	420		
46	630	6	420		

Chapter 10
Practice SAT French
Subject Test 1:
Answers and Explanations

EXPLANATIONS

The possible choices are examined for clues that should have indicated the correct answer. To help explain why a choice is right or wrong, resemblances between English and French words are noted, grammatical explanations are given, and an analysis of the Comprehension questions is provided. Key words in the English translations of the questions are in **boldface**, as are the correct answers.

Part A

Question		Answer	Key Word or Phrase	Fill in
1	I need to do (pack) my . . . before **leaving on vacation** tomorrow.	C	*partir en vacances*	suitcase
2	It's **nice outside**; do you want . . . after dinner?	D	*Il fait beau* (notice that these verbs, used with *te*, are reflexive)	to walk, to go outside
3	The **soldier** waited impatiently for the end of . . .	C	*soldat*	the war
4	It is forbidden to keep your shoes **indoors**; leave them . . .	D	*dans la maison*	outside
5	Paul needs . . . **to hold up his pants.**	D	*soutenir son pantalon*	a belt, suspenders
6	For his **birthday**, the boy received many . . .	D	*anniversaire*	presents
7	I bought . . . **in the bakery** next door.	B	*boulangerie*	bread
8	The . . . of my building is **564.**	C	564	number
9	There are **twelve . . . in a year.**	A	*douze, an*	months
10	The movie theater is **empty**; we can . . . anywhere.	D	*vide*	sit
11	When I wear my favorite **shoes,** I never have sore . . .	B	*souliers*	feet
12	**I agree** with him; I think that he is . . .	B	*d'accord*	right
13	My office is **located** in a different . . . from my apartment.	A	*se trouve*	neighborhood, city, area

Question		Answer	Key Word or Phrase	Fill in
14	The **hero** . . . a girl who was in the process of drowning.	A	*héros*	saved, rescued
15	In summer, one should wear . . . **to protect one's eyes.**	C	*yeux*	glasses (sun)
16	One must pay attention before . . . **the road.**	A	*la rue*	crossing
17	It is **not nice** . . . your friends.	C	*ce n'est pas gentil*	to be mean to, to hurt, to tease
18	The constant **noise** . . .	A	*bruit*	annoys me, upsets me
19	The **waiter** . . . my glass of wine.	A	*serveur*	filled, spilled, brought
20	The lady . . . her **arm to catch the ball.**	A	*bras, attraper*	extended, reached out
21	The student **wrote** . . . on the work of Maupassant.	C	*écrit*	an essay, a paper
22	Without the protection of an umbrella, I will be . . . by the **rain**.	B	*pluie*	soaked

Part B

Question	Category	Answer	Explanation
23	Pronouns	C	(A) no negative to go with *ne* (B) no pronoun to indicate what is being suggested **(C) correct: *ne* plus a negative** (D) *rien* must be used with *ne*
24	Pronouns	B	(A) *que* is never used with a preposition **(B) correct: *qui* can be used with prepositions** (C) which—makes no sense (D) what—makes no sense
25	Odds and Ends: Articles	A	**(A) correct: *homme* is masculine but because it starts with a silent "h" it takes *cet* and not *ce*** (B) *huile* would require *cette* (C) *dame* would require the feminine *cette* (D) *livre* would require the regular masculine *ce*

Question	Category	Answer	Explanation
26	Pronouns	C	The required pronoun needs to refer to place or location. (A) *en* will only refer to location if used with a verb that normally takes *de* (*Vient-il de là-bas? Oui, il en vient.*) (B) *où* meaning "where" is used like *qui* or *que* to connect phrases (C) **correct: *y* refers to place** (D) *là* means "there"
27	Prepositions	C	(A) the correct expression would be *au Mexique* (B) the correct expression would be *en France* (C) **correct: for cities, you use *à*** (D) the correct expression would be *en Chine*
28	Relative Pronouns	C	(A) *de quoi* is an interrogative pronoun when placed at the beginning of a sentence (B) *ce que* is a direct object (C) **correct: *ce dont* is needed with the expression *se plaindre de*** (D) *a quoi* uses the wrong preposition
29	Pronouns	C	(A) subject pronoun (B) indirect object pronoun (C) **correct: stressed pronoun as the object of a preposition** (D) reflexive pronoun
30	Prepositions	A	(A) **correct: *réfléchir* requires *à*** (B) you cannot say *réfléchir sans* (C) you cannot say *réfléchir avec* (D) you cannot use *dont* with *laquelle*
31	Verbs	A	(A) **correct: *vendre* requires *avoir*—"has sold"** (B) *être* would form a passive tense, "is sold"—does not work (C) no need for subjunctive (D) *vendre* requires *avoir*, and there is no need for subjunctive
32	Pronouns	C	(A) *quand* cannot be used after *au moment* (B) *après* is a preposition (C) **correct: *où* is used in expressions of time** (D) *durant* means during, which doesn't fit here

Question	Category	Answer	Explanation
33	Verbs	B	(A) the present doesn't work here since the other action is in the past **(B) correct: imperfect—he was outside in an ongoing way in the past** (C) no need for subjunctive or present (D) no need for conditional
34	Verbs	D	(A) imperfect—cannot follow an imperfect clause beginning with *si* (B) no need for the past conditional (C) the future **(D) correct: if the *si* clause uses the imperfect, the following clause will use the present conditional**
35	Pronouns	D	(A) in this context, *laver* needs to be reflexive (B) *brosser* is used for teeth, not hands (C) *serrer la main*, to shake hands **(D) correct: the expression is *se laver les mains***
36	Prepositions	D	(A) *décider* takes *de* (B) *avoir le droit* takes *de* (C) *avoir envie* takes *de* **(D) correct: *vouloir* takes a direct object**
37	Verbs	A	**(A) correct: *il faut que* requires the subjunctive** (B) present indicative (C) future—wrong tense (D) imperfect—wrong tense
38	Pronouns	B	(A) subject pronoun **(B) correct: stressed pronoun as the object of the preposition** (C) reflexive pronoun (D) indirect object pronoun
39	Verbs	A	**(A) correct: present** (B) no need for subjunctive, as nothing is hypothetical (C) imperfect cannot be used since action has not taken place yet (D) the future is possible but requires *ce—ce sera*

Question	Category	Answer	Explanation
40	Odds and Ends	C	(A) *si difficile* is not a comparative (B) *le meilleur* is a superlative, not a comparative (C) **correct: *pire* can be used to compare two things** (D) *trop* is an adverb that needs to modify a verb, an adjective, or another adverb
41	Prepositions	A	(A) **correct: *durant* means "during"** (B) *sinon* means "otherwise" (C) *afin de* means "in order to" (D) *avant que* must be followed by a clause with a verb
42	Pronouns	C	(A) this leaves the sentence incomplete (B) *tu* would take the verb form *as—tu m'as écrit* (C) **correct: "it is he who"** (D) *personne* requires *ne* in a sentence

Part C

Question	Category	Answer	Explanation
43	Verbs	C	(A) imperfect indicates an ongoing action in the past (B) conditional indicates one thing happening because of another (C) **correct: present** (D) past imperfect indicates an ongoing action that was completed in the past
44	Verbs	A	(A) **correct: no agreement** (B) no need for feminine (C) no need for plural (D) no need for feminine plural
45	Vocabulary	D	(A) past—makes no sense (B) unpleasant (i.e., bad weather)—makes no sense (C) sad—makes no sense (D) **correct: *favorable* (i.e., good weather)**
46	Vocabulary	C	(A) far from (B) never (C) **correct: finally** (D) simply

Question	Category	Answer	Explanation
47	Prepositions	D	(A) you cannot say *partir dans* Tokyo (B) without—makes no sense (C) you cannot say *partir en* Tokyo **(D) correct: *partir pour* Tokyo**
48	Verbs	C	(A) imperfect—wrong tense (B) subjunctive—wrong tense **(C) correct: *qui est née*. Present tense is always used when speaking about birth or death.** (D) wrong person—this is the conjugation for the pronoun "tu," not "ma femme" (elle)
49	Prepositions	B	(A) you cannot say *née en Japon* **(B) correct: *née au Japon* (*Japon* is masculine, so "*au*" is correct, not "*à la*")** (C) you cannot say *née à Japon* (D) you cannot say *née dans Japon*
50	Vocabulary	C	(A) again (B) not again **(C) correct: never** (D) hardly
51	Odds and Ends	D	(A) often (B) sometimes (C) simply **(D) correct: so much**
52	Vocabulary	A	**(A) correct: to attend** (B) to knock down (C) to sit (D) to aspire, to inhale, etc.
53	Vocabulary	B	(A) in spite (of the fact) **(B) correct: because—*parce que*** (C) without (D) as soon as
54	Vocabulary	C	(A) proud (B) annoyed **(C) correct: calm** (D) heavy

Question	Category	Answer	Explanation
55	Vocabulary	D	(A) to get rid of (B) to overflow (C) to develop (D) **correct: to take off**
56	Odds and Ends: Adjectives	A	(A) **correct: past participle or adjective** (B) verb: to study (C) noun: a study (D) noun: a student
57	Vocabulary	D	(A) minutes (B) seconds (C) moments (D) **correct: weeks**
58	Verbs	A	(A) **correct: present—follows *Maintenant*** (B) imperfect (C) conditional (D) *passé composé*

Part D

Question		Answer	Explanation
59	What did the couple do before looking for the café?	B	(A) "They waited." (B) **"They took their car to a garage.": correct—another way of saying *Ayant laissé la voiture au garage . . .*** (C) "They spoke to two children.": familiar words—wrong context (D) "They hit something.": familiar words—wrong context
60	Where is the couple?	D	(A) *À Chartres*: familiar words—wrong context (B) "in a village": *ne formaient pas un village* (C) "in a big town": common sense—if it's not even a village, it's certainly not a city (D) **"in a suburb of the town": correct—key words are *un faubourg lointain***

Question		Answer	Explanation
61	For what reason did the couple go to the café?	D	(A) "to eat a good meal": no, since *Ils commandèrent n'importe quoi pour justifier leur présence.* (B) "to find someone to talk to": no context for this (C) "to ask directions": no context for this (D) **"to pass the time": correct**—*ils décidèrent d'attendre dans un café*
62	What does the author mean by "*l'heure creuse*"?	C	(A) "that there were a lot of people in the café": incorrect—the café was empty (B) "that it was almost night": no context for this (C) **"that no one was there": correct**—*Il n'y avait personne.* (D) "that it was time for the café to close": no context for this
63	What impression did the lady have at the café?	D	(A) "that she had eaten cotton": familiar words—wrong context (B) "that she had on too much makeup": familiar words—wrong context (C) "that there was too much noise": familiar words—wrong context (D) **"that she couldn't hear": correct**—*les bruits ne lui parvenaient qu'assourdis*
64	The author writes in a style that is	C	(A) "serious" (B) "neutral": the author is obviously doing more than just describing the scene (C) **"humorous": correct—tip-offs are word play** (*rangé, se range*), **exaggeration** (D) "scientific"
65	What makes the race car driver appear?	A	(A) **"the act of getting behind the wheel":** *et que réveille le simple contact du pied sur l'accélérateur* (B) "the sunrise" (C) "the action of waking up" (D) "a horn": familiar word—*klaxonner*—but wrong context

Question		Answer	Explanation
66	According to the passage, Jérôme Charnelet is usually	B	(A) "a race car driver": familiar words—wrong context **(B) "of an amiable disposition": correct—*ce bon père de famille . . .*** (C) "impatient" (D) "generous"
67	How does Jérôme react to the green light?	D	(A) "He stops.": makes no sense (B) "He swats a fly.": familiar words—wrong context (C) "He has trouble seeing colors.": you're interpreting too literally **(D) "He becomes a crazy driver.": correct—*il voit rouge***
68	What would convince Jérôme to change his position on the road?	C	(A) "the realization that he is in the middle of the road": familiar words—wrong context (B) "his sense of obligation to the other drivers": familiar words—wrong context **(C) "the horns of other drivers": correct—*après avoir subi une klaxonnade nourrie . . .* "After having been subjected to continuous honking . . . "** (D) "the color of the traffic light": familiar words—wrong context
69	We understand that Jérôme drives in a manner that is	D	(A) "orderly" (B) "steady": familiar word—*rangée*—but wrong context (C) "gracious" **(D) "obsessed": correct—obsédée; the key word is *démoniaque***
70	These apartments	C	(A) "will be renovated in 2005"—no context for this (B) "were renovated in the 19th century"—familiar words—wrong context **(C) "are being renovated": correct—*"en cours de rénovation"*** (D) "are renovated"
71	This advertisement is aimed at	A	**(A) "prospective buyers": correct—*"bureau de vente"*** (B) "future tenants"—no context for this (C) "elderly people"—no context for this (D) "sellers"—familiar word—wrong context

Question	Answer	Explanation
72	After reading this advertisement, one is aware of everything BUT	C	(A) "the proximity of Paris to the residence"—*aux portes de Paris* (B) "the opening hours of the sales office"—*du lundi au samedi de 9 h 30 à 19 h* **(C) "the precise address of the residence": correct—this is the only thing one does not know about these apartments** (D) "the existence of a show apartment"—*appartement-témoin*
73	This passage is concerned with	B	(A) "the number of students in the educational system": incorrect—percentages are given, not numbers **(B) "the attitudes of French adolescents": correct** (C) "the way to change the attitude of French students": no context for this (D) "recent changes in the educational system": no context for this
74	What does the expression "*ils en ont ras le bol*" mean?	D	(A) "that they do not have enough to eat" (B) "that they complain about their studies" (C) "that they should shave" **(D) "that they are sick and tired of something": correct—*ils en ont assez***
75	According to certain students, where does one learn the most?	D	(A) "at home": no context for this (B) "at school": obviously incorrect (C) "in a hierarchy": incorrect—this is one of the problems **(D) "in life": correct—*à la radio, au cinéma, à la télévision ou en voyageant . . .***
76	What is the strongest criticism of the educational system?	C	(A) "There is too much work.": no context for this (B) "The students are bored.": a concern, but not the biggest problem **(C) correct: *l'école est souvent coupée de la vie . . .* "school is often cut off from life . . ."** (D) "There are not enough bosses.": just the opposite

Question		Answer	Explanation
77	The narrator expects	A	(A) "to be scolded by his boss": correct—*j'ai pensé qu'il allait me dire de moins téléphoner et de mieux travailler* (B) "to get a raise": no context for this (C) "to discuss a project with his boss": no context for this (D) "to annoy the boss": familiar words—wrong context
78	What does the boss do?	C	(A) "He annoys the narrator.": familiar words—wrong context (B) "He orders him to go to Paris.": too strong—the boss asks if he wants to go (C) **"He asks what the narrator thinks of a question.": correct—*Il voulait seulement avoir mon avis sur la question*** (D) "He refuses to let the narrator go to Paris.": wrong
79	What does the boss want to do in Paris?	C	(A) "He wants to live there.": perhaps, but too vague to be a good answer (B) "He wants to work for a big company.": familiar words—wrong context (C) **"He wants to open an office.": correct— *l'intention d'installer un bureau à Paris . . .*** (D) "He wishes to betray his company.": no evidence for this
80	Why does the boss suggest the project to the narrator?	B	(A) "because the narrator isn't working well": no, the narrator is evidently being rewarded (B) **"because he thinks the narrator would be happy with such a life": correct—*il me semble que c'est une vie qui doit vous plaire*** (C) "because the boss is too young to do it himself": familiar words—but misleading (D) "because it's all the same to the narrator": familiar words—wrong context
81	What reaction does the narrator have to the idea of going to Paris?	D	(A) "He is irritated.": no context for this (B) "He is happy.": he is neither happy nor unhappy (C) "He feels rejuvenated.": no context for this (D) **"He's not very interested.": correct—*dans le fond cela m'était égal***

Question		Answer	Explanation
82	What makes a river bigger?	B	(A) "an increase in water that comes from the mouth of the river": familiar words—wrong context (B) **"the presence of something that blocks the way": correct—*Quand une rivière est bouchée par une grosse pierre . . .*** (C) "the presence of rocks": familiar words—wrong context (D) "the freedom of water": familiar words—wrong context
83	Why does the author describe a river?	D	(A) "to characterize Trenet's music": not in this case (B) "to explain nature": makes no sense (C) "to show Trenet's importance": tricky—but not an answer to this question (D) **"to make an analogy with the development of song": correct—*Il se passe souvent la même chose dans l'histoire des arts.***
84	It is inferred that before Trenet, the song (in this context, *la chanson* means songs in general)	C	(A) "was more like a river": makes no sense (B) "was more complicated": no context for this (C) **"had fewer possibilities": correct—*après lui les artistes se sentent plus libres . . .*** (D) "was more artistic": no context for this
85	One can infer that Trenet	A	(A) **"introduced a new way of presenting a song": correct—*Charles Trenet a fait sauter ce qui bouchait la chanson française . . .*** (B) "loved nature": makes no sense (C) "wrote a hundred songs": familiar words but wrong context (D) "wasn't liked by other singers": no context for this

Chapter 11
Practice SAT French
Subject Test 2

FRENCH SUBJECT TEST 2

SECTION 2

Your responses to the SAT French questions must be filled in on Section 2 of your answer sheet (at the back of the book). Marks on any other section will not be counted toward your score.

When your supervisor gives the signal, turn the page and begin the SAT French Subject Test.

FRENCH SUBJECT TEST 2

PLEASE NOTE THAT YOUR ANSWER SHEET HAS FIVE ANSWER POSITIONS MARKED A, B, C, D, E, WHILE THE QUESTIONS THROUGHOUT THIS TEST CONTAIN ONLY FOUR CHOICES. BE SURE <u>NOT</u> TO MAKE ANY MARKS IN COLUMN E.

Part A

Directions: This part consists of a number of incomplete statements, each having four suggested completions. Select the most appropriate completion and fill in the corresponding oval on the answer sheet.

1. Il est encore . . . . On va rater le train.

   (A) en avance
   (C) en retard
   (B) à l'heure
   (D) d'accord

2. N'oublie pas ton parapluie, il va . . . ce soir.

   (A) pleurer
   (B) faire froid
   (C) ouvrir
   (D) pleuvoir

3. Il n'y a plus rien dans le réfrigérateur. Il faut que j'aille . . .

   (A) prendre une douche
   (B) tondre le gazon
   (C) faire les courses
   (D) mettre le couvert

4. J'ai mal au . . . . Je vais prendre rendez-vous chez l'orthopédiste.

   (A) nez
   (B) genou
   (C) oreilles
   (D) médecin

5. Sa voiture est toujours en <u>panne</u> et il en a vraiment . . .

   (A) marre
   (B) mer
   (C) miel
   (D) dégoûté

6. Au crépuscule, le ciel . . . de mille feux.

   (A) éteignait
   (B) disparaissait
   (C) tombait
   (D) brillait

7. Il a trouvé très difficile l'examen qu'il a . . . hier.

   (A) passé
   (B) pris
   (C) attrapé
   (D) reçu

8. Jean va acheter des livres à la . . .

   (A) boucherie
   (B) librairie
   (C) pâtisserie
   (D) bibliothèque

9. Elle est si allergique à la poussière qu'elle . . . sans arrêt.

   (A) éclate
   (B) éclabousse
   (C) éternue
   (D) embrasse

10. Il a tout fait pour atteindre son . . .

   (A) test
   (B) travail
   (C) branche
   (D) but

GO ON TO THE NEXT PAGE

11. Il s'est évanoui en apprenant . . .

    (A) la nouvelle — the news
    (B) la leçon
    (C) le fauteuil
    (D) la poubelle

12. Personne ne répond à la porte; elle n'est probablement pas . . .

    (A) là
    (B) dessus
    (C) dessous
    (D) à côté

13. La voiture . . . net devant l'enfant qui traversait la rue en courant.

    (A) s'emporta
    (B) s'assura
    (C) s'arrêta
    (D) s'écria

14. Ils ont choisi d'habiter . . . avec leurs trois petits enfants.

    (A) en banlieue
    (B) en chemin
    (C) en cachette
    (D) en retard

15. Ils sont pleins d'énergie et sont . . . tous les matins à 6 heures.

    (A) étendus
    (B) assis
    (C) debout
    (D) fâchés

16. Ne sachant que faire, j'ai demandé . . . à mon avocat.

    (A) conseil
    (B) contribution
    (C) contact
    (D) compagnie

17. Pour son entrevue avec son futur employeur demain, elle va mettre . . .

    (A) un soulier
    (B) un tailleur — suit
    (C) un costume
    (D) un portemanteau

18. Elle a . . . beaucoup d'argent pour acheter sa maison.

    (A) prêté
    (B) renversé
    (C) emprunté — borrow
    (D) vendu

19. Pour faire ce gâteau, vous . . . de beaucoup de sucre.

    (A) avez envie
    (B) avez besoin
    (C) avez soif
    (D) avez peur

20. Il est exténué; il a . . . travaillé.

    (A) peu
    (B) bientôt
    (C) souvent
    (D) trop

21. Les trains passent moins souvent les jours . . .

    (A) normaux
    (B) libres
    (C) fériés — holidays
    (D) courants

22. Les alpinistes vont . . . l'ascension du Mont Kilimandjaro.

    (A) modifier
    (B) montrer
    (C) tirer
    (D) tenter

GO ON TO THE NEXT PAGE

23. Des années d'usage vont . . . le cuir de ces bottes.

   (A) assiéger
   (B) réduire
   (C) assouplir
   (D) surprendre

24. Si je pars maintenant, je peux . . . les embouteillages.

   (A) estimer
   (B) revoir
   (C) arranger
   (D) éviter

GO ON TO THE NEXT PAGE

Part B

Directions: Each of the following sentences contains a blank. From the four choices given, select the one that can be inserted in the blank to form a grammatically correct sentence and fill in the corresponding oval on the answer sheet. Choice (A) may consist of dashes that indicate that no insertion is required to form a grammatically correct sentence.

25. Le livre ------- j'ai perdu hier est à mon frère.

    (A) dont
    (B) à qui
    (C) que
    (D) lequel

26. Je suis passée à la maison ------- prendre mon parapluie.

    (A) à
    (B) pour
    (C) parce que
    (D) après

27. Mon père revenait toujours ------- à la maison entre midi et deux heures.

    (A) déjeuner
    (B) déjeuné
    (C) déjeunait
    (D) déjeunant

28. Elle est rentrée ------- Danemark hier soir.

    (A) de
    (B) du
    (C) en
    (D) aux

29. Elle dessine beaucoup ------- que son frère.

    (A) bien
    (B) meilleur
    (C) mal
    (D) mieux

30. La robe qu'elle a ------- hier n'est vraiment pas à la mode.

    (A) mise
    (B) acheté
    (C) mis
    (D) enfiler

31. Il ne sera pas là demain ------- il vient de partir en voyage d'affaires.

    (A) bien qu'
    (B) avant qu'
    (C) puisqu'
    (D) à moins qu'

32. Regarde ------- tu mets les pieds quand tu marches.

    (A) là
    (B) où
    (C) vers
    (D) près de

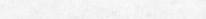
GO ON TO THE NEXT PAGE

33. Appelle-moi ------- prendre une décision.

    (A) en
    (B) pendant
    (C) avant de
    (D) à

34. Bien que ------- débordée de travail, j'essaierai de passer te voir ce soir.

    (A) j'étais *imp*
    (B) je serais *cont*
    (C) je sois *sub*
    (D) je suis

35. Est-ce que tu veux un bonbon? Oui, j'en veux bien -------.

    (A) quelque
    (B) peu
    (C) un peu
    (D) un

36. Est-ce que Marie est déjà partie à la poste? Non, mais elle va ------- aller tout de suite.

    (A) y
    (B) en
    (C) toujours
    (D) demain

37. Si elle s'entraînait plus sérieusement, elle ------- toutes les courses.

    (A) gagnerait
    (B) gagnait
    (C) gagnera
    (D) a gagné

38. Il faut que ------- à la banque demain matin pour retirer de l'argent.

    (A) j'allais
    (B) j'aille
    (C) j'irai
    (D) j'irais

GO ON TO THE NEXT PAGE

Part C

Directions: The paragraphs below contain blank spaces indicating omissions in the text. For some blanks, it is necessary to choose the completion that is most appropriate to the meaning of the passage; for other blanks, to choose the one completion that forms a grammatically correct sentence. In some instances, choice (A) may consist of dashes that indicate that no insertion is required to form a grammatically correct sentence. In each case, indicate your answer by filling in the corresponding oval on the answer sheet. Be sure to read the paragraph completely before answering the questions related to it.

Il n'avait pas mangé ----(39)---- le matin. Les cafés qu'il rencontrait à ----(40)---- pas l'intimidaient et ----(41)---- dégoûtaient, à cause de la foule qui ----(42)---- était ----(43)----. Il s'adressa ----(44)---- un gendarme. Mais il était si lent à ----(45)---- ses mots que l'autre ne se donna même pas la peine de l'écouter ----(46)---- bout et lui tourna ----(47)----, au milieu de la phrase, en ----(48)---- les épaules. Il continua machinalement ----(49)---- marcher.

39. (A) après
    (B) depuis
    (C) pour
    (D) dans

40. (A) tous
    (B) chacun
    (C) chaque
    (D) quelque

41. (A) lui
    (B) la
    (C) le
    (D) leur

42. (A) en
    (B) y
    (C) dans
    (D) où

43. (A) entassé
    (B) entasser
    (C) entassées
    (D) entassée

44. (A) à
    (B) vers
    (C) avec
    (D) pour

45. (A) trouvé
    (B) trouver
    (C) trouvés
    (D) trouvait

46. (A) à travers
    (B) jusque-là
    (C) au
    (D) jusqu'au

47. (A) la tête
    (B) le dos ~ back
    (C) l'oreille
    (D) les yeux

48. (A) tirant
    (B) portant
    (C) haussant
    (D) passant

49. (A) -------
    (B) pour
    (C) à
    (D) en

GO ON TO THE NEXT PAGE

Cher Monsieur,

La lettre ----(50)---- je vous ----(51)---- adressée le 1er juillet ----(52)---- restée sans réponse, je me permets de vous écire pour ----(53)---- prier de prendre ma requête ----(54)---- considération.

50. (A) -------
    (B) laquelle
    (C) dont
    (D) que

51. (A) aie
    (B) ai
    (C) aurai
    (D) avait

52. (A) ayant
    (B) avant
    (C) étant
    (D) était

53. (A) te
    (B) me
    (C) vous
    (D) le

54. (A) en
    (B) avec
    (C) par
    (D) comme

Quand j'étais petit, mes parents ----(55)---- emmenaient ----(56)---- nager à la piscine municipale de Roubaix.

55. (A) leur
    (B) te
    (C) s'
    (D) m'

56. (A) peut-être
    (B) pourtant
    (C) une fois
    (D) souvent

GO ON TO THE NEXT PAGE

Part D

Directions: Read the following texts carefully for comprehension. Each is followed by a number of questions or incomplete statements. Select the completion or answer that is best according to the text and fill in the corresponding oval on the answer sheet.

"L'été est trop long," disait la grand-mère qui accueillait du même soupir soulagé la pluie d'automne et le départ de Jacques, dont les piétinements d'ennui
Ligne au long des journées torrides, dans les pièces aux
5 persiennes closes, ajoutaient encore à son énervement.
Elle ne comprenait pas d'ailleurs qu'une période de l'année fût plus spécialement désignée pour n'y rien faire. "Je n'ai jamais eu de vacances, moi," disait-elle, et c'était vrai, elle n'avait connu ni l'école
10 ni le loisir, elle avait travaillé enfant, et travaillé sans relâche. Elle admettait que, pour un bénéfice plus grand, son petit-fils pendant quelques années ne rapporte pas d'argent à la maison. Mais, dès le premier jour, elle avait commencé de ruminer sur
15 ces trois mois perdus, et, lorsque Jacques entra en troisième, elle jugea qu'il était temps de lui trouver l'emploi de ses vacances. "Tu vas travailler cet été," lui dit-elle à la fin de l'année scolaire,"et rapporter un peu d'argent à la maison. Tu ne peux pas rester
20 comme ça sans rien faire."

(Albert Camus, *Le premier homme*, Folio)

57. Quand arrivait la pluie d'automne, la grand-mère était

   (A) énervée
   (B) triste
   (C) contente ~ glad
   (D) fière

58. Pendant les mois d'été, Jacques

   (A) travaillait beaucoup
   (B) passait son temps à lire
   (C) s'amusait sans arrêt
   (D) ne savait comment se distraire

59. Quand elle était petite, la grand-mère

   (A) avait de moins longues vacances que Jacques
   (B) dessinait pendant ses loisirs
   (C) passait tout son temps au travail
   (D) ne faisait jamais rien

60. D'après le texte, on comprend que

   (A) Jacques poursuit ses études
   (B) la grand-mère ne veut pas que Jacques aille encore à l'école
   (C) la grand-mère refuse que Jacques travaille pendant l'été
   (D) Jacques est le troisième de sa classe

61. La grand-mère veut que Jacques ait un emploi pour qu'il

   (A) ait un peu d'argent de poche
   (B) puisse payer ses études
   (C) contribue aux dépenses de la famille
   (D) apprenne un métier

GO ON TO THE NEXT PAGE

Avant de venir au Central, lisait-il, je viens d'assister à une scène d'une atroce beauté.

Ligne

On a trouvé cette nuit près de la Puerta del Sol un enfant de trois ans qui pleurait perdu, dans les
5   ténèbres. Or, une des femmes réfugiées dans les sous-sols de la Gran Via ignorait ce qu'était devenu son enfant, un petit garçon du même âge, blond comme l'enfant trouvé dans la Puerta del Sol. On lui donne la nouvelle. Elle court à la maison où l'on garde l'enfant,
10 calle Montera. Dans la demi-obscurité d'une boutique aux rideaux baissés, l'enfant suce un morceau de chocolat. La mère s'avance vers lui, les bras tendus, mais ses yeux s'agrandissent, prennent une fixité terrible, démente.
15 Ce n'est pas son enfant.

Elle reste immobile de longues minutes. L'enfant perdu lui sourit. Alors elle se précipite sur lui, le serre contre elle, l'emporte en pensant à l'enfant qu'on n'a pas retrouvé.

(André Malraux, *L'espoir*, Folio Plus)

62. L'enfant de trois ans pleure parce qu'

(A) il a perdu son morceau de chocolat
(B) il s'est fait mal
(C) il ne sait pas où est sa famille
(D) il fait nuit

63. Les rideaux de la boutique sont

(A) ouverts
(B) levés
(C) descendus
(D) déchirés

64. La femme "se précipite sur lui" veut dire qu'elle va vers l'enfant

(A) en courant
(B) à pas lents
(C) en pleurant
(D) avec nonchalance

65. Elle "le serre contre elle" signifie qu'elle

(A) le repousse
(B) l'embrasse
(C) lui sourit
(D) le frappe

66. A qui la femme pense-t-elle en emportant l'enfant?

(A) A son propre fils
(B) Au fils d'une des refugiées
(C) Au fils du lecteur
(D) Au fils d'un garde

GO ON TO THE NEXT PAGE →

TRAIN + VOITURE: EN TOUTE LIBERTÉ

Evitez les bouchons des grands départs!

En choisissant la formule "Train + Location de voitures," vous êtes sûrs de bénéficier de tous les avantages: le confort du train, la liberté de la voiture … Tout en réalisant de vraies **économies**!

Pratique: à la descente du train, votre voiture vous attend en gare.

Economique: vous bénéficiez d'une réduction importante sur votre location.

Efficace: vous réservez votre voiture en même temps que votre train.

Pour profiter de cette offre:

– Réservez votre place.

– En fin de commande, cliquez sur "AJOUTER UNE VOITURE."

– Choisissez l'offre "Train + Location de Voitures."

67. Les bouchons dont il est question dans le texte

    (A) servent à boucher les bouteilles

    (B) sont des embouteillages

    (C) retardent les trains

    (D) évitent de perdre du temps

68. D'après le texte, la solution Train + Location de Voitures

    (A) revient plus cher

    (B) coûte trop cher

    (C) n'est guère pratique

    (D) est une bonne affaire

GO ON TO THE NEXT PAGE

Ligne

Les Français auraient-ils attrapé le virus du home cinéma ? A en croire la grande majorité des constructeurs d'électronique grand public, la réponse ne fait pas de doute. Les équipements liés au cinéma
5 à domicile, qui englobent aussi bien de la hi-fi que de la vidéo, ont le vent en poupe. Tous les professionnels du secteur s'accordent même pour dire que 2002 devrait être l'année de l'explosion de ce marché en France. Près de 4 millions de téléviseurs, dont 15%
10 avec un écran au format cinéma 16/9, devraient ainsi être vendus en 2002 selon les prévisions de l'institut GFK.

"Il y a toujours eu en France une forte sensibilité des gens à consommer des films à la maison,"
15 explique Jean-Marc Auffret, responsable marketing home cinéma chez Sony France. "Mais jusqu'à présent le home cinéma était réservé à une frange très cinéphile et relativement aisée financièrement. Aujourd'hui, avec l'apparition des appareils combinés
20 et la baisse des prix de certains éléments audiovisuels, le grand public peut plus facilement s'équipper." Il est sans doute encore trop tôt pour parler de démocratisation—installer un ensemble home cinéma coûte toujours entre 1300 et plus de 60000 euros selon
25 les matériels choisis—mais les constructeurs disposent de plus en plus de produits abordables. Aujourd'hui, il est possible d'acheter un ensemble composé d'un lecteur de DVD équipé d'un amplificateur et d'un pack de six enceintes pour moins de 700 euros.

(Guillaume Fraissard, *Le Monde*, 31 mai, 2002)

69. D'après cet article, les Français

(A) vont de plus en plus souvent au cinéma
(B) vont rarement au cinéma
(C) préfèrent regarder la télévision
(D) aiment de plus en plus regarder des films chez eux

70. Les équipements liés au cinéma à domicile

(A) ont de plus en plus de succès
(B) ne sont pas nouveaux
(C) n'ont guère d'intérêt
(D) ne sont pas dans le vent

71. Aujourd'hui, l'audiovisuel est

(A) plus coûteux
(B) meilleur marché
(C) hors de prix
(D) inabordable

72. "Le grand public" représente

(A) quelques privilégiés
(B) les gens célèbres
(C) les amateurs de cinéma
(D) la plupart des gens

73. " . . . les constructeurs disposent de plus en plus de produits abordables" signifie qu'ils

(A) s'en débarrassent
(B) en ont besoin
(C) y ont accès
(D) en fabriquent

GO ON TO THE NEXT PAGE ➤

Voici la recette des madeleines, ces petits gâteaux de forme ovale au ventre bombé, si chers à Marcel Proust:

La veille, mélangez soigneusement les ingrédients suivants jusqu'à l'obtention d'une pâte parfaitement lisse:

Madeleines

Farine	90 gr
Sucre	90 gr
Levure	2 gr
Miel de Provence	10 gr
Oeufs	2
Beurre fondu	90 gr
Le zeste d'un citron	
Pastis (facultatif)	1 cl

Conservez cette pâte au réfrigérateur.

Le lendemain, distribuez la pâte dans 12 moules à madeleines beurrés. Enfournez à four moyen et laissez cuire jusqu'à ce que les gâteaux aient une belle couleur dorée. Démoulez sur une grille à la sortie du four, laissez refroidir, et dégustez!

74. Quand faut-il préparer la pâte des madeleines?

(A) Le lendemain
(B) Le jour précédent
(C) Deux heures à l'avance
(D) Hier

75. D'après la recette, le pastis est un ingrédient

(A) indispensable
(B) sucré
(C) optionnel
(D) parfumé

GO ON TO THE NEXT PAGE

Le bossu reparut, une brochure à la main. Il s'installa commodément, les coudes sur la table, son menton entre ses mains.

Ligne
"Je vous ai déjà laissé entendre, dit-il, que j'avais
5 des projets d'une assez grande envergure."

"De vastes projets."

"C'est cela même, et je vais vous les révéler aujourd'hui." Il prit le ton d'un conférencier.

"Ce qui m'a attiré ici, c'est d'abord mon amour
10 de la nature. Mais quoique je ne manque pas d'argent en ce moment, j'ai une famille à nourrir, et je dois assurer l'avenir de ma fillette: c'est pourquoi le philosophe que je suis a voulu concilier son désir de la vie naturelle et l'obligation où il se trouve de faire
15 fortune."

De ce discours, Ugolin ne retint que les derniers mots. Il avait l'intention de "faire fortune." Faire fortune aux Romarins! Avec quoi? Sûrement pas avec ces oliviers à demi morts, ni ces amandiers à l'agonie;
20 ni avec des légumes, ni avec du blé, ni avec du vin. Il connaissait donc la source, et il voulait peut-être planter des oeillets! C'est pourquoi, par une contre-attaque désespérée, il dit: "Vous savez ici, les fleurs, même si vous aviez une belle source . . ."
25 "Quelles fleurs?" dit le bossu d'un air surpris. "Croyez-vous que j'espère faire fortune en vendant des églantines ou des chardons? Et quelle source? Vous savez que celle que je possède est bien loin d'ici!"

(Marcel Pagnol, *Jean de Florette*, Presses Pocket)

76. "Je vous ai déjà laissé entendre" signifie "je vous ai déjà"

(A) dit
(B) répété
(C) suggéré
(D) menti

77. Le bossu a de "vastes projets" parce qu'il

(A) a besoin d'argent tout de suite
(B) pense à l'avenir de sa fille
(C) est philosophe
(D) aime beaucoup l'argent

78. Du discours du bossu, Ugolin se souvient

(A) uniquement des derniers mots
(B) peut-être des premiers mots
(C) toujours de la dernière phrase
(D) de tout sauf de la fin

79. Aux lignes 18–23, apres l'annonce des projets du bossu, Ugolin est

(A) amusé
(B) très inquiet
(C) rempli de joie
(D) rassuré

80. Ugolin cherche à savoir si le bossu

(A) va planter des vignes
(B) va sauver les oliviers et les amandiers
(C) compte vendre des chardons
(D) connaît l'existence de la source

GO ON TO THE NEXT PAGE

Ligne

Vous comprenez tout de suite que la vraie ville est l'arsenal, que l'autre ne vit que par lui, qu'il déborde sur elle. Sous toutes les formes, en tous lieux, à tous les coins réapparaissent l'administration, la discipline,

5 la feuille de papier rayé, le cadre, la règle. On admire beaucoup la symétrie factice et la propreté imbécile. A l'hôpital de la marine, par exemple, les salles sont cirées de telle façon qu'un convalescent, essayant de marcher sur sa jambe remise, doit se casser l'autre

10 en tombant. Mais c'est beau, ça brille, on s'y mire. Entre chaque salle est une cour, mais où le soleil ne vient jamais et dont soigneusement on arrache l'herbe. Les cuisines sont superbes, mais à une telle distance, qu'en hiver tout doit parvenir glacé aux malades. Il

15 s'agit bien d'eux! Les casseroles ne sont-elles pas luisantes? Nous vîmes un homme qui s'était cassé le crâne en tombant d'une frégate et qui depuis dix-huit heures n'avait pas encore reçu de secours; mais ses draps étaient très blancs, car la lingerie est fort bien

20 tenue.

(Gustave Flaubert, *Notes de voyage*, L'Intégrale)

81. "En tous lieux" signifie

(A) nulle part
(B) partout
(C) ailleurs
(D) quelque part

82. Le convalescent risque de se casser l'autre jambe parce que le sol est

(A) mouillé
(B) inégal
(C) plein de trous
(D) glissant

83. La cour entre chaque salle est

(A) inondée de soleil
(B) privée d'ombre
(C) ensoleillée
(D) privée de soleil

84. En hiver les repas sont servis aux malades

(A) brûlants
(B) tièdes
(C) à point
(D) très froids

85. Le ton de Flaubert dans ce passage est

(A) sarcastique
(B) sérieux
(C) enjoué
(D) tragique

S T O P
IF YOU FINISH BEFORE TIME IS CALLED, YOU MAY CHECK YOUR WORK ON THIS TEST ONLY.
DO NOT WORK ON ANY OTHER TEST IN THIS BOOK.

HOW TO SCORE THE PRINCETON REVIEW
FRENCH SUBJECT TEST

When you take the real exam, the proctors will collect your test booklet and bubble sheet and send your answer sheet to New Jersey where a computer looks at the pattern of filled-in ovals on your answer sheet and gives you a score. We are providing you, however, with this more primitive way of scoring your exam.

Determining Your Score

STEP 1   Using the answers on the next page, determine how many questions you got right and how many you got wrong on the test. Remember, questions that you do not answer do not count as either right answers or wrong answers.

STEP 2   Write the number of correct answers on line A.   (A) _____

STEP 3   Write the number of wrong answers on line B. Divide   (B) _____ ÷ 3 = _____
          that number by 3.

STEP 4   Subtract the number of wrong answers divided by 3   (A) _____ – (B) _____ = (C) _____
          on line B from the number of correct answers on line
          A, and round to the nearest whole number. (C) is your
          raw score.

STEP 5   To determine your **real score**, look up your raw score
          in the left column of the Score Conversion Table on
          page 218; the corresponding score on the right is the
          score you earned on the exam.

ANSWERS TO FRENCH SUBJECT TEST 2

Question number	Correct answer	Right	Wrong	Question number	Correct answer	Right	Wrong	Question number	Correct answer	Right	Wrong
1.	C	___	___	36.	A	___	___	71.	B	___	___
2.	D	___	___	37.	A	___	___	72.	D	___	___
3.	C	___	___	38.	B	___	___	73.	C	___	___
4.	B	___	___	39.	B	___	___	74.	B	___	___
5.	A	___	___	40.	C	___	___	75.	C	___	___
6.	D	___	___	41.	C	___	___	76.	C	___	___
7.	A	___	___	42.	B	___	___	77.	B	___	___
8.	B	___	___	43.	D	___	___	78.	A	___	___
9.	C	___	___	44.	A	___	___	79.	B	___	___
10.	D	___	___	45.	B	___	___	80.	D	___	___
11.	A	___	___	46.	D	___	___	81.	B	___	___
12.	A	___	___	47.	B	___	___	82.	D	___	___
13.	C	___	___	48.	C	___	___	83.	D	___	___
14.	A	___	___	49.	C	___	___	84.	D	___	___
15.	C	___	___	50.	D	___	___	85.	A	___	___
16.	A	___	___	51.	B	___	___				
17.	B	___	___	52.	C	___	___				
18.	C	___	___	53.	C	___	___				
19.	B	___	___	54.	A	___	___				
20.	D	___	___	55.	D	___	___				
21.	C	___	___	56.	D	___	___				
22.	D	___	___	57.	C	___	___				
23.	C	___	___	58.	D	___	___				
24.	D	___	___	59.	C	___	___				
25.	C	___	___	60.	A	___	___				
26.	B	___	___	61.	C	___	___				
27.	A	___	___	62.	C	___	___				
28.	B	___	___	63.	C	___	___				
29.	D	___	___	64.	A	___	___				
30.	A	___	___	65.	B	___	___				
31.	C	___	___	66.	A	___	___				
32.	B	___	___	67.	B	___	___				
33.	C	___	___	68.	D	___	___				
34.	C	___	___	69.	D	___	___				
35.	D	___	___	70.	A	___	___				

THE PRINCETON REVIEW FRENCH SUBJECT TEST
SCORE CONVERSION TABLE

Raw score	Scaled score	Raw score	Scaled score	Raw score	Scaled score
85	800	45	630	5	410
84	800	44	620	4	410
83	800	43	620	3	400
82	800	42	610	2	400
81	800	41	610	1	390
80	800	40	600	0	390
79	800	39	600	−1	380
78	800	38	590	−2	380
77	800	37	580	−3	370
76	790	36	580	−4	360
75	790	35	570	−5	360
74	780	34	570	−6	350
73	780	33	560	−7	350
72	770	32	560	−8	340
71	770	31	550	−9	340
70	760	30	550	−10	330
69	760	29	540	−11	330
68	750	28	540	−12	320
67	740	27	530	−13	320
66	740	26	530	−14	310
65	730	25	520	−15	300
64	730	24	520	−16	290
63	720	23	510	−17	290
62	720	22	500	−18	280
61	710	21	500	−19	280
60	710	20	490	−20	270
59	700	19	490	−21	270
58	700	18	480	−22	260
57	690	17	480	−23	260
56	690	16	470	−24	250
55	680	15	470	−25 through −28	240
54	680	14	460		
53	670	13	460		
52	660	12	450		
51	660	11	450		
50	650	10	440		
49	650	9	430		
48	640	8	430		
47	640	7	420		
46	630	6	420		

Chapter 12
Practice SAT French Subject Test 2: Answers and Explanations

EXPLANATIONS

The possible choices are examined for clues that should have indicated the correct answer. To help explain why a choice is right or wrong, resemblances between English and French words are noted, grammatical explanations are given, and an analysis of the comprehension questions is provided. Key words in the English translations of the questions are in **boldface**, as are the correct answers.

Part A

Question		Answer	Key Word or Phrase	Fill In
1	He is . . . again. We are going to miss the train.	C	*rater le train*	late
2	Don't forget your umbrella; it's going to . . . tonight.	D	*parapluie*	rain
3	There's nothing left in the refrigerator. I have to . . .	C	*il n'y a plus rien*	go shopping
4	I have a pain in my . . . . I'm going to make an appointment with the orthopedist.	B	*orthopédiste*	knee
5	His car keeps breaking down and he is really . . .	A	*est toujours en panne*	fed up
6	At dusk the sky . . . with a thousand lights.	D	*de mille feux*	sparkled
7	He found the test he . . . yesterday very hard.	A	*l'examen*	took
8	Jean is going to buy books at the . . .	B	*acheter*	bookstore
9	She is so allergic to dust that she . . . repeatedly.	C	*allergique*	sneezes
10	He has done everything to reach his . . .	D	*atteindre*	goal
11	He fainted when he heard . . .	A	*apprenant*	the news
12	Nobody is answering the door; she is probably not . . .	A	*personne ne répond*	there

Question		Answer	Key Word or Phrase	Fill In
13	The car . . . dead in front of the child who was running across the street.	C	*voiture*	stopped
14	They have chosen to live . . . with their three young children.	A	*habiter*	in the suburbs
15	They are full of energy and are . . . every morning at 6.	C	*Ils sont pleins d'énergie*	up
16	Not knowing what to do, I asked my lawyer for . . .	A	*ne sachant que faire*	advice
17	For her interview with her future boss tomorrow, she is going to wear . . .	B	*elle va mettre*	suit
18	She has . . . a lot of money to buy her house.	C	*beaucoup d'argent*	borrowed
19	In order to make this cake, you . . . a lot of sugar.	B	*pour faire ce gâteau*	need
20	He is exhausted; he has worked . . .	D	*exténué*	too much
21	The trains will **run less often** on. . . days.	C	*passent moins souvent*	holidays
22	The **mountain climbers** are going to . . . **a climb** of Mount Kilimanjaro.	D	*alpinistes, ascension*	attempt, try
23	**Years of use** will . . . **the leather** of these boots.	C	*années d'usage, cuir*	break in, wear out, soften
24	If I leave now, I can . . . **traffic jams**.	D	*les embouteillages*	avoid, miss

Part B

Question	Category	Answer	Explanation
25	Pronouns	C	(A) whose—*perdre* takes a direct object (B) to whom—*perdre* takes a direct object and a book is not a person **(C) correct—which, right answer because *que* is a direct object pronoun** (D) when it is not an interrogative pronoun, *lequel* can only be used with a preposition, i.e., *avec lequel, pour lequel*
26	Prepositions	B	(A) at **(B) correct—*pour*, here, means "in order to"** (C) because (D) after
27	Verbs	A	**(A) correct—the infinitive is required when a verb follows another verb** (B) past participle—grammatically incorrect (C) imperfect—grammatically incorrect (D) present participle—grammatically incorrect
28	Prepositions	B	(A) *Danemark* is masculine; *de* in this case can only be used with a feminine country, i.e., *de France, de Belgique* **(B) correct—*Danemark* is masculine** (C) *en* could only work with a feminine country, i.e., *en France, en Suisse* (D) *aux* is plural—grammatically incorrect
29	Adverbs	D	(A) the adverb *beaucoup* cannot be used before *bien* (B) the adverb *beaucoup* cannot be used before *meilleur* (C) makes no sense **(D) correct—*mieux*, the comparative form of *bien*, may be preceded by *beaucoup***
30	Past Participles	A	**(A) correct—the verb *mettre* takes *avoir*, so the past participle agrees with the direct object *robe*, placed before the verb** (B) grammatically incorrect—no past participle agreement (C) grammatically incorrect—no past participle agreement (D) grammatically incorrect—infinitive
31	Conjunctions	C	(A) although: followed by the subjunctive form of the verb (B) before: followed by the subjunctive form of the verb **(C) correct—since, *puisque*, is followed by the indicative form of the verb** (D) unless: followed by the subjunctive form of the verb

Question	Category	Answer	Explanation
32	Adverbs	B	(A) there **(B) correct—where** (C) toward (D) near
33	Prepositions	C	(A) in (B) during **(C) correct—before** (D) at
34	Subjunctive	C	(A) I was: imperfect—wrong tense (B) I would be: conditional—wrong tense **(C) correct—subjunctive required after *bien que*** (D) I am: present—wrong tense
35	Pronouns	D	(A) makes no sense because *quelque* is not a pronoun (B) little—makes no sense (C) a little—*un peu* is used with something that is not numbered, i.e., *un peu de vin, de lait, de salade* . . . It would therefore be used after a question such as, *Est-ce que tu veux du vin, du lait, de la salade . . . ?* **(D) correct— "one," *un* is used as a pronoun here**
36	Pronouns	A	**(A) correct—*y* replaces *à la poste*, which is a place** (B) from there—*en* makes no sense with the verb *aller*; it can be used with *venir*: *j'en viens* (C) always—makes no sense (D) tomorrow—makes no sense
37	Conditional	A	**(A) correct— "would win": present conditional is required after *si elle s'entraînait*** (B) won: imperfect—wrong tense (C) will win: future—wrong tense (D) has won: *passé composé*—wrong tense
38	Subjunctive	B	(A) I went: imperfect—wrong tense **(B) correct—subjunctive of the verb *aller* required after *il faut que*** (C) I will go: future—wrong tense (D) I would go: conditional—wrong tense

Part C

Question	Category	Answer	Explanation
39	Vocabulary	B	(A) after—makes no sense **(B) correct—since** (C) for—makes no sense (D) in—*dans* is not used before *le matin*
40	Adjectives	C	(A) all—would require the article *les* (B) each one—makes no sense **(C) correct—every** (D) some—makes no sense
41	Pronouns	C	(A) grammatically wrong—*lui* is never a direct object (B) grammatically wrong—*la* refers to *elle*, not *il* **(C) correct—*le* is masculine and a direct object** (D) grammatically wrong—*leur* is indirect and plural
42	Pronouns	B	(A) from there—*en* makes no sense here **(B) correct—*y* refers to *les cafés*** (C) in—makes no sense (D) where—makes no sense
43	Past Participles	D	(A) grammatically wrong—masculine ending (B) grammatically wrong—infinitive (C) grammatically wrong—plural feminine ending **(D) correct—refers to *la foule*, which is feminine and singular**
44	Prepositions	A	**(A) correct—*s'adresser* takes *à* and means *parler à*** (B) toward—inappropriate (C) with—makes no sense (D) for—makes no sense
45	Verbs	B	(A) grammatically incorrect—past participle **(B) correct—the infinitive is used after a preposition** (C) grammatically incorrect—plural past participle (D) grammatically incorrect—imperfect

Question	Category	Answer	Explanation
46	Prepositions	D	(A) through—makes no sense (B) up to here—makes no sense (C) at the—makes no sense (D) correct—"to the end"; *bout* is a masculine noun and therefore needs the article *le. Jusqu'à* becomes *jusqu'au—jusqu'à* followed by a feminine noun would be *jusqu'à la* as in *jusqu'à la fin.*
47	Vocabulary	B	(A) head (B) correct—back (C) ear (D) eyes
48	Vocabulary	C	(A) pulling (B) carrying (C) correct—shrugging (D) passing
49	Prepositions	C	(A) ------- *continuer* requires a preposition (B) for (C) correct—*continuer à* (D) in
50	Relative Pronouns	D	(A) ------- in French you may not omit a relative pronoun or a conjunction such as "that" or "which" in English (B) literally, the which (C) whose—*dont* is wrong because *adresser* takes a direct object: *adresser une lettre* (D) correct—direct object relative pronoun
51	Verbs	B	(A) subjunctive not needed here (B) correct—*adresser* takes *avoir* and the correct tense is the *passé composé* in the first person (C) will have—the future makes no sense here (D) had—*avait*, wrong tense, wrong person
52	Present Participles	C	(A) wrong verb—need *être*, not *avoir* (B) before—makes no sense (C) correct—*rester* takes *être*; with a causative clause, you need the present participle (D) was—makes no sense in the context

Question	Category	Answer	Explanation
53	Pronouns	C	(A) wrong—a formal letter requires *vous* (B) me—this would refer back to the speaker **(C) correct** (D) him—there is no third party in the sentence
54	Prepositions	A	**(A) correct—the French expression is *prendre en consideration*** (B) with (C) by (D) as
55	Pronouns	D	(A) wrong: *leur* is an indirect object pronoun, while *emmener* takes a direct object (B) wrong: *emmener* starts with a vowel (C) makes no sense because *emmener* is not a reflexive verb **(D) correct—refers to the narrator; *emmener* starts with a vowel and the *m'* is required**
56	Vocabulary	D	(A) maybe (B) yet (C) once—wrong because imperfect **(D) correct—often**

Part D

Question		Answer	Explanation
57	When the autumn rain arrived, the grandmother was	C	(A) "edgy" (B) "sad" (C) **correct: "glad"**—*accueillait du même soupir soulagé la pluie d'automne*—the grandmother "welcomed the autumn rain with the same sigh of relief" (D) "proud"
58	During the summer months, Jacques	D	(A) "worked a lot"—familiar words, wrong context (B) "spent his time reading"—no mention of reading in the text (C) "never stopped having fun"—on the contrary, the text refers to Jacques's *ennui* (D) **correct: "did not know how to entertain himself"**—key words *piétinements d'ennui*
59	When she was a little girl, the grandmother	C	(A) "had shorter vacations than Jacques"—she had no vacation at all: *Je n'ai jamais eu de vacances, moi.* (B) "used to draw pictures during her free time"—no context for this (C) **correct: "spent all her time working"**—*elle avait travaillé enfant, et travaillé sans relâche* (D) "never did anything"—wrong: *elle avait travaillé sans relâche*

Question		Answer	Explanation
60	According to the passage, we understand that	A	(A) **correct: "Jacques continues his studies"**—*lorsque Jacques entra en troisième* (B) "the grandmother does not want Jacques to keep going to school"—*Elle admettait que, pour un bénéfice plus grand, son petit-fils pendant quelques années ne rapporte pas d'argent à la maison.*—"She agreed that for a greater benefit, her grandson would not bring home any money for a few years." (C) "the grandmother is opposed to Jacques's having a summer job"—no, since she says *Tu vas travailler cet été.* (D) "Jacques is the third in his class"—familiar words—wrong context
61	The grandmother wants Jacques to have a job so that he	C	(A) "might have some pocket money"—no context for this (B) "might be able to pay for his studies"—no context for this (C) **correct: "might contribute to the family expenses"**—*rapporter un peu d'argent à la maison*—"bring home some money" (D) "might learn a trade:"—no context for this
62	The three-year-old child is crying because	C	(A) "he has lost his piece of chocolate" (B) "he has hurt himself" (C) **correct: "he does not know where his family is"**—*perdu*: lost (D) "it is dark"
63	The shutters of the store are	C	(A) "open" (B) "up" (C) **correct: *baissés*—"pulled down"** (D) "torn"
64	The woman "rushes to him" means that she goes toward the child	A	(A) **correct: "running"** (B) "slowly" (C) "crying" (D) "unconcerned"
65	She "presses him tightly against her" means that she	B	(A) "pushes him away" (B) **correct: "hugs him"** (C) "smiles at him" (D) "hits him"

Question		Answer	Explanation
66	Who does the woman think of as she carries the child away?	A	(A) correct: "her own son"—*en pensant à l'enfant qu'on n'a pas retrouvé* (B) "the son of one of the refugees" (C) "the reader's son" (D) "the son of a guard"
67	The traffic jams mentioned in the text	B	(A) "are used to cork a bottle"—double meaning of the word *bouchon*, either a cork or a traffic jam (B) **correct: "are traffic jams"—a street is *embouteillée* when it is jammed with cars** (C) "delay the trains" (D) "avoid wasting time"
68	According to the text, the combination Train + Car Rental	D	(A) "is more expensive" (B) "is too expensive" (C) "is not very convenient" (D) **correct: "is a good deal"—*Tout en réalisant de vraies économies!***
69	According to this article, the French	D	(A) "go to the movies more and more often" (B) "seldom go to the movies" (C) "would rather watch television" (D) **correct: "enjoy watching movies at home more and more"—*Les Français auraient-ils attrapé le virus du home cinéma?* "Have the French caught the home-theater virus?"**
70	The equipment linked to the home theater	A	(A) **correct: "have more and more success"—*2002 devrait être l'année de l'explosion de ce marché en France*—"2002 should be the booming year of this market in France"** (B) "are not new" (C) "are not very interesting" (D) "are not in"—*être dans le vent* is a French idiom meaning *être à la mode*

Question		Answer	Explanation
71	Today, audiovisual equipment is	B	(A) "more expensive" (B) **correct: "cheaper"**—*la baisse des prix*: **lower prices** (C) "exorbitant"—literally "out of price" (D) "prohibitive"—literally "that cannot be reached"
72	"The general public" represents	D	(A) "a few privileged people" (B) "famous people" (C) "film enthusiasts" (D) **correct: "most people"**
73	". . . the manufacturers have more and more affordable products at their disposal" means that they	C	(A) "are getting rid of them" (B) "need them" (C) **correct: "have access to them"—watch out!** *Disposer de* **here does not mean "to dispose of" but "to have at one's disposal."** —i.e., *Je dispose de 1000 pour m'acheter un ordinateur* **means "I have 1000 euros at my disposal to buy a computer."** (D) "make them"
74	When do you have to prepare the dough for the madeleines?	B	(A) "the next day" (B) **correct: "the day before"**—*la veille*: **the day before** (C) "two hours ahead of time" (D) "yesterday"
75	According to the recipe, pastis is an ingredient which is	C	(A) "a must" (B) "sweet" (C) **correct: "optional"**—*facultatif* (D) "fragrant"
76	"I have already hinted to you that" means "I have already"	C	(A) "told you" (B) "repeated to you" (C) **correct: "suggested to you"** (D) "lied to you"

Question		Answer	Explanation
77	The hunchback has "big plans" because	B	(A) "he needs money right away" (B) correct: "he thinks about his daughter's future"—*je dois assurer l'avenir de ma fillette*: "I have to secure my little girl's future" (C) "he is a philosopher" (D) "he loves money"
78	From the hunchback's speech, Ugolin remembers	A	(A) correct: "only the last words"—*De ce discours, Ugolin ne retint que les derniers mots. Ne . . . que* means "only." (B) "maybe the first words" (C) "always the last sentence" (D) "everything but the end"
79	In lines 18–23, after hearing the hunchback's plans, Ugolin is	B	(A) "amused" (B) correct: "very worried" (C) "full of joy" (D) "reassured"
80	Ugolin is trying to find out whether the hunchback	D	(A) "is going to plant a vineyard" (B) "will save the olive trees and the almond trees" (C) "is planning to sell thistles" (D) correct: "knows about the existence of the spring"—*il connaissait donc la source*: "so he knew about the spring"
81	"In every place" means	B	(A) "nowhere" (B) correct: "everywhere" (C) "somewhere else" (D) "somewhere"
82	The convalescent runs the risk of breaking his other leg because the floor is	D	(A) "wet" (B) "uneven" (C) "full of holes" (D) correct: "slippery"—*les salles sont cirées de telle façon qu'un convalescent, . . . doit se casser l'autre en tombant*—"the rooms are waxed in such a way that a convalescent . . . must fall and break the other one"

Question		Answer	Explanation
83	The courtyard in between every room is	D	(A) "full of sun" (B) "without any shade" (C) "sunny" (D) correct: "without any sun"—*mais où le soleil ne vient jamais*: "but where the sun never comes"
84	In winter the patients' meals are	D	(A) "piping hot" (B) "lukewarm" (C) "at the right temperature" (D) correct: "very cold"—*tout doit parvenir glacé*: icy cold
85	Flaubert's tone in this passage is	A	(A) correct: "sarcastic"—Flaubert describes what he calls *la symétrie factice* ("the artificial symmetry") and *la propreté imbécile* ("the stupid cleanliness") of the arsenal (B) "serious" (C) "playful" (D) "tragic"

About the Authors

Monique Gaden, a graduate of the Université de Lyon, and Simone Ingram, a graduate of the Université de Lille, have taught French and English for many years. They have collaborated on the revision of this book and on the creation of the second practice test.

Practice Test 1 Form

Completely darken bubbles with a No. 2 pencil. If you make a mistake, be sure to erase mark completely. Erase all stray marks.

1.

YOUR NAME: _____
(Print)   Last   First   M.I.

SIGNATURE: _____   DATE: ___/___/___

HOME ADDRESS: _____
(Print)   Number and Street

_____
City   State   Zip Code

(Print)

Section 1

1. Ⓐ Ⓑ Ⓒ Ⓓ Ⓔ	26. Ⓐ Ⓑ Ⓒ Ⓓ Ⓔ	51. Ⓐ Ⓑ Ⓒ Ⓓ Ⓔ	76. Ⓐ Ⓑ Ⓒ Ⓓ Ⓔ
2. Ⓐ Ⓑ Ⓒ Ⓓ Ⓔ	27. Ⓐ Ⓑ Ⓒ Ⓓ Ⓔ	52. Ⓐ Ⓑ Ⓒ Ⓓ Ⓔ	77. Ⓐ Ⓑ Ⓒ Ⓓ Ⓔ
3. Ⓐ Ⓑ Ⓒ Ⓓ Ⓔ	28. Ⓐ Ⓑ Ⓒ Ⓓ Ⓔ	53. Ⓐ Ⓑ Ⓒ Ⓓ Ⓔ	78. Ⓐ Ⓑ Ⓒ Ⓓ Ⓔ
4. Ⓐ Ⓑ Ⓒ Ⓓ Ⓔ	29. Ⓐ Ⓑ Ⓒ Ⓓ Ⓔ	54. Ⓐ Ⓑ Ⓒ Ⓓ Ⓔ	79. Ⓐ Ⓑ Ⓒ Ⓓ Ⓔ
5. Ⓐ Ⓑ Ⓒ Ⓓ Ⓔ	30. Ⓐ Ⓑ Ⓒ Ⓓ Ⓔ	55. Ⓐ Ⓑ Ⓒ Ⓓ Ⓔ	80. Ⓐ Ⓑ Ⓒ Ⓓ Ⓔ
6. Ⓐ Ⓑ Ⓒ Ⓓ Ⓔ	31. Ⓐ Ⓑ Ⓒ Ⓓ Ⓔ	56. Ⓐ Ⓑ Ⓒ Ⓓ Ⓔ	81. Ⓐ Ⓑ Ⓒ Ⓓ Ⓔ
7. Ⓐ Ⓑ Ⓒ Ⓓ Ⓔ	32. Ⓐ Ⓑ Ⓒ Ⓓ Ⓔ	57. Ⓐ Ⓑ Ⓒ Ⓓ Ⓔ	82. Ⓐ Ⓑ Ⓒ Ⓓ Ⓔ
8. Ⓐ Ⓑ Ⓒ Ⓓ Ⓔ	33. Ⓐ Ⓑ Ⓒ Ⓓ Ⓔ	58. Ⓐ Ⓑ Ⓒ Ⓓ Ⓔ	83. Ⓐ Ⓑ Ⓒ Ⓓ Ⓔ
9. Ⓐ Ⓑ Ⓒ Ⓓ Ⓔ	34. Ⓐ Ⓑ Ⓒ Ⓓ Ⓔ	59. Ⓐ Ⓑ Ⓒ Ⓓ Ⓔ	84. Ⓐ Ⓑ Ⓒ Ⓓ Ⓔ
10. Ⓐ Ⓑ Ⓒ Ⓓ Ⓔ	35. Ⓐ Ⓑ Ⓒ Ⓓ Ⓔ	60. Ⓐ Ⓑ Ⓒ Ⓓ Ⓔ	85. Ⓐ Ⓑ Ⓒ Ⓓ Ⓔ
11. Ⓐ Ⓑ Ⓒ Ⓓ Ⓔ	36. Ⓐ Ⓑ Ⓒ Ⓓ Ⓔ	61. Ⓐ Ⓑ Ⓒ Ⓓ Ⓔ	
12. Ⓐ Ⓑ Ⓒ Ⓓ Ⓔ	37. Ⓐ Ⓑ Ⓒ Ⓓ Ⓔ	62. Ⓐ Ⓑ Ⓒ Ⓓ Ⓔ	
13. Ⓐ Ⓑ Ⓒ Ⓓ Ⓔ	38. Ⓐ Ⓑ Ⓒ Ⓓ Ⓔ	63. Ⓐ Ⓑ Ⓒ Ⓓ Ⓔ	
14. Ⓐ Ⓑ Ⓒ Ⓓ Ⓔ	39. Ⓐ Ⓑ Ⓒ Ⓓ Ⓔ	64. Ⓐ Ⓑ Ⓒ Ⓓ Ⓔ	
15. Ⓐ Ⓑ Ⓒ Ⓓ Ⓔ	40. Ⓐ Ⓑ Ⓒ Ⓓ Ⓔ	65. Ⓐ Ⓑ Ⓒ Ⓓ Ⓔ	
16. Ⓐ Ⓑ Ⓒ Ⓓ Ⓔ	41. Ⓐ Ⓑ Ⓒ Ⓓ Ⓔ	66. Ⓐ Ⓑ Ⓒ Ⓓ Ⓔ	
17. Ⓐ Ⓑ Ⓒ Ⓓ Ⓔ	42. Ⓐ Ⓑ Ⓒ Ⓓ Ⓔ	67. Ⓐ Ⓑ Ⓒ Ⓓ Ⓔ	
18. Ⓐ Ⓑ Ⓒ Ⓓ Ⓔ	43. Ⓐ Ⓑ Ⓒ Ⓓ Ⓔ	68. Ⓐ Ⓑ Ⓒ Ⓓ Ⓔ	
19. Ⓐ Ⓑ Ⓒ Ⓓ Ⓔ	44. Ⓐ Ⓑ Ⓒ Ⓓ Ⓔ	69. Ⓐ Ⓑ Ⓒ Ⓓ Ⓔ	
20. Ⓐ Ⓑ Ⓒ Ⓓ Ⓔ	45. Ⓐ Ⓑ Ⓒ Ⓓ Ⓔ	70. Ⓐ Ⓑ Ⓒ Ⓓ Ⓔ	
21. Ⓐ Ⓑ Ⓒ Ⓓ Ⓔ	46. Ⓐ Ⓑ Ⓒ Ⓓ Ⓔ	71. Ⓐ Ⓑ Ⓒ Ⓓ Ⓔ	
22. Ⓐ Ⓑ Ⓒ Ⓓ Ⓔ	47. Ⓐ Ⓑ Ⓒ Ⓓ Ⓔ	72. Ⓐ Ⓑ Ⓒ Ⓓ Ⓔ	
23. Ⓐ Ⓑ Ⓒ Ⓓ Ⓔ	48. Ⓐ Ⓑ Ⓒ Ⓓ Ⓔ	73. Ⓐ Ⓑ Ⓒ Ⓓ Ⓔ	
24. Ⓐ Ⓑ Ⓒ Ⓓ Ⓔ	49. Ⓐ Ⓑ Ⓒ Ⓓ Ⓔ	74. Ⓐ Ⓑ Ⓒ Ⓓ Ⓔ	
25. Ⓐ Ⓑ Ⓒ Ⓓ Ⓔ	50. Ⓐ Ⓑ Ⓒ Ⓓ Ⓔ	75. Ⓐ Ⓑ Ⓒ Ⓓ Ⓔ	

Practice Test 2 Form

Completely darken bubbles with a No. 2 pencil. If you make a mistake, be sure to erase mark completely. Erase all stray marks.

1.

YOUR NAME: _____
(Print)   Last   First   M.I.

SIGNATURE: _____   DATE: ___ / ___ / ___

HOME ADDRESS: _____
(Print)   Number and Street

_____
            City   State   Zip Code

(Print)

Section 2

1. Ⓐ Ⓑ Ⓒ Ⓓ Ⓔ	26. Ⓐ Ⓑ Ⓒ Ⓓ Ⓔ	51. Ⓐ Ⓑ Ⓒ Ⓓ Ⓔ	76. Ⓐ Ⓑ Ⓒ Ⓓ Ⓔ
2. Ⓐ Ⓑ Ⓒ Ⓓ Ⓔ	27. Ⓐ Ⓑ Ⓒ Ⓓ Ⓔ	52. Ⓐ Ⓑ Ⓒ Ⓓ Ⓔ	77. Ⓐ Ⓑ Ⓒ Ⓓ Ⓔ
3. Ⓐ Ⓑ Ⓒ Ⓓ Ⓔ	28. Ⓐ Ⓑ Ⓒ Ⓓ Ⓔ	53. Ⓐ Ⓑ Ⓒ Ⓓ Ⓔ	78. Ⓐ Ⓑ Ⓒ Ⓓ Ⓔ
4. Ⓐ Ⓑ Ⓒ Ⓓ Ⓔ	29. Ⓐ Ⓑ Ⓒ Ⓓ Ⓔ	54. Ⓐ Ⓑ Ⓒ Ⓓ Ⓔ	79. Ⓐ Ⓑ Ⓒ Ⓓ Ⓔ
5. Ⓐ Ⓑ Ⓒ Ⓓ Ⓔ	30. Ⓐ Ⓑ Ⓒ Ⓓ Ⓔ	55. Ⓐ Ⓑ Ⓒ Ⓓ Ⓔ	80. Ⓐ Ⓑ Ⓒ Ⓓ Ⓔ
6. Ⓐ Ⓑ Ⓒ Ⓓ Ⓔ	31. Ⓐ Ⓑ Ⓒ Ⓓ Ⓔ	56. Ⓐ Ⓑ Ⓒ Ⓓ Ⓔ	81. Ⓐ Ⓑ Ⓒ Ⓓ Ⓔ
7. Ⓐ Ⓑ Ⓒ Ⓓ Ⓔ	32. Ⓐ Ⓑ Ⓒ Ⓓ Ⓔ	57. Ⓐ Ⓑ Ⓒ Ⓓ Ⓔ	82. Ⓐ Ⓑ Ⓒ Ⓓ Ⓔ
8. Ⓐ Ⓑ Ⓒ Ⓓ Ⓔ	33. Ⓐ Ⓑ Ⓒ Ⓓ Ⓔ	58. Ⓐ Ⓑ Ⓒ Ⓓ Ⓔ	83. Ⓐ Ⓑ Ⓒ Ⓓ Ⓔ
9. Ⓐ Ⓑ Ⓒ Ⓓ Ⓔ	34. Ⓐ Ⓑ Ⓒ Ⓓ Ⓔ	59. Ⓐ Ⓑ Ⓒ Ⓓ Ⓔ	84. Ⓐ Ⓑ Ⓒ Ⓓ Ⓔ
10. Ⓐ Ⓑ Ⓒ Ⓓ Ⓔ	35. Ⓐ Ⓑ Ⓒ Ⓓ Ⓔ	60. Ⓐ Ⓑ Ⓒ Ⓓ Ⓔ	85. Ⓐ Ⓑ Ⓒ Ⓓ Ⓔ
11. Ⓐ Ⓑ Ⓒ Ⓓ Ⓔ	36. Ⓐ Ⓑ Ⓒ Ⓓ Ⓔ	61. Ⓐ Ⓑ Ⓒ Ⓓ Ⓔ	
12. Ⓐ Ⓑ Ⓒ Ⓓ Ⓔ	37. Ⓐ Ⓑ Ⓒ Ⓓ Ⓔ	62. Ⓐ Ⓑ Ⓒ Ⓓ Ⓔ	
13. Ⓐ Ⓑ Ⓒ Ⓓ Ⓔ	38. Ⓐ Ⓑ Ⓒ Ⓓ Ⓔ	63. Ⓐ Ⓑ Ⓒ Ⓓ Ⓔ	
14. Ⓐ Ⓑ Ⓒ Ⓓ Ⓔ	39. Ⓐ Ⓑ Ⓒ Ⓓ Ⓔ	64. Ⓐ Ⓑ Ⓒ Ⓓ Ⓔ	
15. Ⓐ Ⓑ Ⓒ Ⓓ Ⓔ	40. Ⓐ Ⓑ Ⓒ Ⓓ Ⓔ	65. Ⓐ Ⓑ Ⓒ Ⓓ Ⓔ	
16. Ⓐ Ⓑ Ⓒ Ⓓ Ⓔ	41. Ⓐ Ⓑ Ⓒ Ⓓ Ⓔ	66. Ⓐ Ⓑ Ⓒ Ⓓ Ⓔ	
17. Ⓐ Ⓑ Ⓒ Ⓓ Ⓔ	42. Ⓐ Ⓑ Ⓒ Ⓓ Ⓔ	67. Ⓐ Ⓑ Ⓒ Ⓓ Ⓔ	
18. Ⓐ Ⓑ Ⓒ Ⓓ Ⓔ	43. Ⓐ Ⓑ Ⓒ Ⓓ Ⓔ	68. Ⓐ Ⓑ Ⓒ Ⓓ Ⓔ	
19. Ⓐ Ⓑ Ⓒ Ⓓ Ⓔ	44. Ⓐ Ⓑ Ⓒ Ⓓ Ⓔ	69. Ⓐ Ⓑ Ⓒ Ⓓ Ⓔ	
20. Ⓐ Ⓑ Ⓒ Ⓓ Ⓔ	45. Ⓐ Ⓑ Ⓒ Ⓓ Ⓔ	70. Ⓐ Ⓑ Ⓒ Ⓓ Ⓔ	
21. Ⓐ Ⓑ Ⓒ Ⓓ Ⓔ	46. Ⓐ Ⓑ Ⓒ Ⓓ Ⓔ	71. Ⓐ Ⓑ Ⓒ Ⓓ Ⓔ	
22. Ⓐ Ⓑ Ⓒ Ⓓ Ⓔ	47. Ⓐ Ⓑ Ⓒ Ⓓ Ⓔ	72. Ⓐ Ⓑ Ⓒ Ⓓ Ⓔ	
23. Ⓐ Ⓑ Ⓒ Ⓓ Ⓔ	48. Ⓐ Ⓑ Ⓒ Ⓓ Ⓔ	73. Ⓐ Ⓑ Ⓒ Ⓓ Ⓔ	
24. Ⓐ Ⓑ Ⓒ Ⓓ Ⓔ	49. Ⓐ Ⓑ Ⓒ Ⓓ Ⓔ	74. Ⓐ Ⓑ Ⓒ Ⓓ Ⓔ	
25. Ⓐ Ⓑ Ⓒ Ⓓ Ⓔ	50. Ⓐ Ⓑ Ⓒ Ⓓ Ⓔ	75. Ⓐ Ⓑ Ⓒ Ⓓ Ⓔ	

NOTES

NOTES

NOTES

NOTES

NOTES

NOTES

NOTES

Our Books Help You Navigate the College Admissions Process

AP Exams

**Cracking the AP Biology Exam,
2009 Edition**
978-0-375-42884-5 • $18.00/C$21.00

**Cracking the AP Calculus AB & BC Exams,
2009 Edition**
978-0-375-42885-2 • $19.00/C$22.00

**Cracking the AP Chemistry Exam,
2009 Edition**
978-0-375-42886-9 • $18.00/C$22.00

**Cracking the AP Computer Science A & AB,
2006–2007**
978-0-375-76528-5 • $19.00/C$27.00

**Cracking the AP Economics Macro & Micro
Exams, 2009 Edition**
978-0-375-42887-6 • $18.00/C$21.00

**Cracking the AP English Language &
Composition Exam, 2009 Edition**
978-0-375-42888-3 • $18.00/C$21.00

**Cracking the AP English Literature &
Composition Exam, 2009 Edition**
978-0-375-42889-0 • $18.00/C$21.00

**Cracking the AP Environmental
Science Exam, 2009 Edition**
978-0-375-42890-6 • $18.00/C$21.00

**Cracking the AP European History Exam,
2009 Edition**
978-0-375-42891-3 • $18.00/C$21.00

**Cracking the AP Physics B Exam,
2009 Edition**
978-0-375-42892-0 • $18.00/C$21.00

**Cracking the AP Physics C Exam,
2009 Edition**
978-0-375-42893-7 • $18.00/C$21.00

**Cracking the AP Psychology Exam,
2009 Edition**
978-0-375-42894-4 • $18.00/C$21.00

**Cracking the AP Spanish Exam,
with Audio CD, 2009 Edition**
978-0-375-76530-8 • $24.95/$27.95

**Cracking the AP Statistics Exam,
2009 Edition**
978-0-375-42848-7 • $19.00/C$22.00

**Cracking the AP U.S. Government
and Politics Exam, 2009 Edition**
978-0-375-42896-8 • $18.00/C$21.00

**Cracking the AP U.S. History Exam,
2009 Edition**
978-0-375-42897-5 • $18.00/C$21.00

**Cracking the AP World History Exam,
2009 Edition**
978-0-375-42898-2 • $18.00/C$21.00

SAT Subject Tests

**Cracking the SAT Biology E/M Subject Test,
2009–2010 Edition**
978-0-375-42905-7 • $19.00/C$22.00

**Cracking the SAT Chemistry Subject Test,
2009–2010 Edition**
978-0-375-42906-4 • $19.00/C$22.00

**Cracking the SAT French Subject Test,
2009–2010 Edition**
978-0-375-42907-1 • $19.00/C$22.00

**Cracking the SAT U.S. & World History
Subject Tests, 2009–2010 Edition**
978-0-375-42908-8 • $19.00/C$22.00

**Cracking the SAT Literature Subject Test,
2009–2010 Edition**
978-0-375-42909-5 • $19.00/C$22.00

**Cracking the SAT Math 1 & 2 Subject Tests,
2009–2010 Edition**
978-0-375-42910-1 • $19.00/C$22.00

**Cracking the SAT Physics Subject Test,
2009–2010 Edition**
978-0-375-42911-8 • $19.00/C$22.00

**Cracking the SAT Spanish Subject Test,
2009–2010 Edition**
978-0-375-42912-5 • $19.00/C$22.00

The Princeton Review

Don't Stop Now

We've got even more great info online.

PrincetonReview.com offers an array of online tools to help you prepare for various college admissions exams. The Princeton Review represents the very best in test preparation, and we're committed to ensuring that you have the tools you need to succeed.

More Test Prep—If you're looking to excel on your SAT, ACT, SAT Subject Tests, or AP exams, you're in the right place. We offer private tutoring, small group tutoring, classroom courses, and online courses, as well as various other books to help you prepare.

More Practice—If you need to get ready for the SAT or ACT and you prefer independent study and want a flexible schedule, we recommend one of our online courses. *Online Private Tutoring* for the SAT is our most personalized and comprehensive online option. Our *LiveOnline*, *Online*, or *ExpressOnline* options for the SAT and ACT will help you prepare when and where you need.

More Books—If you like this book, you might want to check out some other books we offer:

    The Best 368 Colleges
    Cracking the ACT
    College Matchmaker
    Complete Book of Colleges

More Fat Envelopes—We know more than just tests. We know a lot about college admissions, too. We'll help you find the school that best meets your needs.

To learn more about any of our private tutoring programs, Small Group Tutoring, classroom courses, or online courses, call **800-2Review** (800-273-8439) or visit **PrincetonReview.com**